MYSTERIOUS SAHARA

SAHARA

THE LAND OF GOLD, OF SAND, AND OF RUIN

By Byron Khun De Prorok, F.R.G.S.

Officier d'Academie - Officier de l'Instruction publique

THE NARRATIVE PRESS

TRUE FIRST-PERSON HISTORICAL ACCOUNTS

To my friends, the heroic Sir Ernest Shackleton,
and Captain Roald Amundsen,
and to my companions of Saharan exploration
who are no more.

I never see a map but I'm away
On all the errands that I long to do
Up all the rivers that are painted blue,
And all the ranges that are painted gray,
And into those pale spaces where they say - "Unknown". . .

The Narrative Press
P.O. Box 2487, Santa Barbara, California 93120 U.S.A.
Telephone: (800) 315-9005 Web: www.narrativepress.com

ISBN 1-58976-257-6 (Paperback)

Produced in the United States of America

COUNT BYRON KHUN DE PROROK

Fellow of the Royal Geographical Society of England and the American, French and Egyptian Geographical Societies; Member of the International Anthropological Institute; Officier d'Academie; Norton Memorial Lecturer of the Archeological Institute of America; Officier de l'Instruction Publique (France) Officer of the Order of Nichem Hitgar (Tunis) Order of Alexandre, etc.

Excavator of ancient Carthage; explorer of the dead cities of North Africa; leader of notable expeditions to the Sahara and Libyan Deserts.

LECTURE SUBJECT:

Illustrated with marvelous still and motion pictures

Exclusive Management of LEE KEEDICK, 475 Fifth Avenue, New York City

TABLE OF CONTENTS

EDITOR'S INTRODUCTION

Mysterious Sahara: Land of Gold, of Sand, and of Ruin, originally published in 1929, was de Prorok's second book. Its main focus is the 1925 expedition into the Algerian Sahara and his late 1920s work in Libya. Here the romantic possibilities of archaeology and exploration are edging out the scientific. All the same, he does a nice job of condensing the history of Saharan exploration and relations between the French and the Tuareg. He even provides footnotes and a bibliography—scholarly details largely absent from his other three books. For a more thorough, and less sensational, history of this subject see Douglas Porch's masterful *Conquest of the Sahara* (1984). For a parallel, and again less sensational, account of the trip to Tamanrasset and Abalessa and the recovery of the skeleton of "Tin Hinan" see Alonzo Pond's *Veiled Men, Red Tents, and Black Mountains,* recently published by The Narrative Press.

Well reviewed when it originally appeared, *Mysterious Sahara* is Byron at his tale spinning best. He had truly hit his stride as a raconteur by this time and the reader gets some sense of the dynamism attributed to him in reviews of his lectures. Missing from most copies of this book, in its beautiful first printing, is the dust jacket with one of Byron's North African watercolors (he supplied another for the frontispiece) and this bit of back cover puffery about our "unusually clever 'personal press agent'":

Count Byron Khun de Prorok, author, explorer, artist, and lecturer, was born with the venturesome spirit of the wanderer and began his distinguished and sensational career at an early age. Fired by the achievements of illustrious predecessors, many of whom, including Sir Ernest Shackleton, were his personal friends, he commenced his researches in remote, dangerous corners of the earth before he reached the age of 25.

The astonishing compass of his activities includes the Rhine and Carpathian Mountains, the ruins of Mexico, the Everglades of Florida, the sites of prehistoric cave-dwellings in Switzerland and the dolmens and megalithic remains in Cornwall and Brittany. Thus seasoned by experience, vigorous and wide in scope, it is not strange that his recent expeditions in Northern Africa— the mysterious Sahara—have brought him world-wide recognition and a solid fame based upon the scientific value of his discoveries.

His excavation of the tomb of Queen Tin Hinan ranks as one of the most important of all Saharan finds. Though he has traveled far with danger and close to the hand of death, he retains the high, fresh spirit of the adventurer and an undiminished eagerness to seek the fascination of the unknown. To his sense of humor and great personal charm his work bears ample testimony. He is now 34 years old.

Crowning this purple prose, in profile pose, is an inspiring, pith-helmeted portrait of the author as a young explorer, shown at the start of this edition.

INTRODUCTION

An author may have a variety of reasons for writing a foreword to his book, but, however warmly he may embrace and cherish these reasons, they carry no weight to those readers who turn lightly through all prefatory remarks on the theory (it may be supposed) that nothing of interest ever is found in the first few pages.

The author's purpose in this case is not to confuse the reader with a skeleton-like outline upon which the meat is to be hung, but to acknowledge here the burden of his debt to those who have been both his helpers and his ever-present source of inspiration. Sincere gratitude is not a freshet-fed spring that bubbles lightly into words; rather is it a deep well that waters the deep growing roots of friendship. Yet I would be remiss in my obligations should I fail to make acknowledgment to those who have aided me so materially.

My first interest in exploration dates from school days, from an afternoon spent with Sir Ernest Shackleton, the Antarctic hero, who inspired a youngster's heart by his friendship and great-hearted sympathy. Later Roald Amundsen took the place of Sir Ernest, who died on "The Quest" amid the storms of the South Atlantic. Both are gone to explore new worlds, but in many an hour spent by the camp fires amid the great sand dunes and vast spaces of the Sahara, I have lingered over the memory of my two gallant friends. It is to their help and inspiration that I owe my career of exploration and the realization of leading expeditions into the heart of that land of gold, of sand, and of ruin.

Of course, my expeditions could not have been undertaken without the help and collaboration of the French, American, Egyptian and British Geographical Societies, of the French and Egyptian Government officials, and of such personal friends as Professor Reygasse of Algiers, Mr. G. P. Putnam, Mr. F. Singer, Mr. Robert Lansing, Mr. Mitchell Carrol, R. P. Bovier-Lapierre, Professor Kelsey of the University of Michigan, Major Shorey, Captain Hillier of Cairo, the Resident Governors of Algeria and Tunisia, as well as the kindly interest of H. M. King Fuad, of Egypt.

However, looking backward now I can definitely place my finger upon the one single incident that doubtlessly changed the course of my life stream. How vividly I recall that summer afternoon on a cricket field in old England when, in company with a group of hero-worshiping boys, I met Sir Ernest Shackleton and listened, openmouthed, to his mighty tales of adventure. Even then I was seized with a fierce longing to accompany the explorer, and my disappointment in not being "taken along" was softened somewhat by his asking me to help raise enough money to buy a sled and its equipment.

For the next several weeks I begged for my god, and I was a proud and happy lad when at last I was able to send him the few funds collected for one of his explorations. He, in return, later sent me a fragment of one of the sleds – *my* sled – which had reached the then "Farthest South."

The lure of discovery and dreams of treasure hunting are ever present in the heart of a boy, and many hours of my youthful days were spent in digging into the mounds known as "Caesar's Camp" above the chalk cliffs of Folkestone. One day a Roman coin appeared – and since that magic day the lure of discovery has led me to the distant lands where sand-buried civilizations have been uncovered and many others are still to be discovered and explored.

In my wanderings first came Rome and Pompeii; then the high Alps; then Mexico with its jungles and ancient temples; then the isles of Greece, and finally – Africa! Carthage, with her classic past; North Africa, with its dead cities and Saharan civilizations when my eyes first beheld the splendors of those places I knew my life work was there.

It is now ten years since our research work began in Africa. Ten years of organizing expeditions; of raising funds; (a task for which few explorers are suited and which, by some Providence, should be lifted from them) of exploring the unmapped wastes of the Sahara; delving into the time-hidden secrets of curse-ridden Carthage – Carthage with its Temple of Tanit and its fearful human sacrifices; ancient Utica, with its golden Punic Tombs; sea-buried Tipasa; our life with the heroic deep sea divers, who gave immeasurable aid in the work at Tipasa; Bulla Regia, the African Pompeii, with its subterranean palaces; the Atlas Mountains and their prehistoric caves; and always in the background the Sahara with its desert mysteries and legends of lost civilizations.

The beauty of the Sahara and of the golden cities is indeed hard to describe, and my first efforts in depicting this land of romance and of color were with the palette and brush. My rudimentary education in water color painting was had at the age of nine at the hands of a kindly gentleman who used to pay yearly visits to the sun-blessed coasts of Southern France. Twelve years later this friend of my youth was greatly astonished when I invited him and his charming wife to open an exhibition of my paintings of North Africa in the Corcoran Gallery at Washington. I was honored by his assent, for my tutor had become a world figure – the beloved and illustrious statesman, Robert Lansing. Since that occasion Mr. Lansing, as President of the Archaeological Society of Washington, several times presented me at lectures at the National Museum at Washington.

Mr. Lansing, Professor Kelsey and Dr. Mitchell Carroll were the leading organizers and advisors of the Franco-American Expedition to North Africa, and words are inadequate to express my gratitude to these splendid men, who helped so generously, and constantly maintained their confidence in the objectives of a young man. The death of these gentlemen was an immeasurable loss to me and to the great work they had sponsored. My early companions in the field, too, are gone. Prince Egard de Waldeck, Professor Jules Renault, Dr. Louis Carton and Lieutenant Estienne have passed on, but their memory will remain forever with me and I feel very close to them whenever I traverse the desert trails we followed together.

Another of these brilliant co-workers is Professor M. Reygasse, the famous African Pre-Historian of the University of Algiers, often an inspiring companion on Saharan trails. And my debt is great to Mr. Stephen Gsell, African Historian of the Institute de France, as well as to that eminent scholar, Professor Gautier, whose advice and knowledge have been invaluable.

My thoughts turn also to the Geographical Societies that have been interested in desert exploration; to Mr. Hinks of the Royal Geographical Society; to Mr. Isaiah Bowman, director of the American Geographical Society; to Mr. Grandidier and Mr. Reiseler of the French National Geographical Society, and to Dr. Meunier and Father Bovier-Lapierre, of the Royal Egyptian Geographical Society.

The chief authorities consulted in this publication are indicated in the bibliography and the footnotes, but special acknowledgment is here due to Mr. F. R. Rodd's "People of the Veil," to Mr. O. Bates' "The Eastern Libyans" and to Mr. S. Gsell for his "Histoire Ancienne de l' Afrique du Nord."

My sincere thanks are also due to Mr. Clarke Venable for his great help in putting together this narration from the accumulation of many years of sand-filled Saharan note books.

To my wife, companion on my recent expedition into the Libyan Desert, with its privations and hardships, and of the subsequently hardly less strenuous lecture tour of America, I offer my deep and sincere admiration.

Chapter 1

MARTYRS OF THE SAHARA

"Far hence he lies,
Near some lone desert town,
And on his grave, with shining eyes,
The Southern stars look down. . . "'

– Mathew Arnold.

The common fate of many men and women who dedicate their lives to some ideal is to die unrewarded and unsung. Since earliest youth, we have heard stories and legends of the Sahara, the world's greatest desert, but how few of us know anything of its glamorous history or of the hundreds of valiant lives that have been sacrificed in its exploration and conquest.

To the majority of the white races the name Sahara presents a picture of illimitable sand wastes, broken here and there by palm-fringed oases, and known and traveled only by roving bands of Arabs. We think of it as a land unchanged by the steady march of centuries; we speak of it as the unconquerable. But in truth it has known an ancient and mighty civilization, and to-day the Saharan trails are marked by many forgotten and untended mounds that indicate the last resting places of heroic explorers who, attempting to lift the veil of Time obscuring the dawn of history, perished in the desert wastes. Some died of thirst, many from madness, but the majority fell before the knives, lances and guns of the dreaded Tuareg. The face of the Sahara is spotted with pathetic sand-blistered crosses, testifying to the courage of explorers, soldiers, or missionaries who gave up their lives in these desolate, far-flung outposts of civilization. The list of these martyrs of the Sahara is indeed long. The roll is not yet ended, nor is the sad epic of endeavor and death in those dreary wastes yet terminated.

The vast, challenging Sahara still is claiming its victims; though it is alluring, majestic, full of wonder and of mystery, it is pitiless to the unwary, the inexperienced, the unprepared. Death strikes swiftly in this dead land, and always when one is least prepared. The scorching sand storm comes up with awful suddenness, equalled only by the silent, swift surprise attack of the desert marauders who swoop down at dawn. But the terror of the Sahara is thirst. Thirst is the brooding shadow of dread that hovers over every caravan, and the dim trails are marked with bleached skeletons of man and beast, victims of this cruel end amid the eternal, mocking sands.

Centuries ago, when travelers and merchants and masters of caravans were safely housed at the end of adventurous journeyings, they regaled eager listeners with desert stories that have become the fireside property of a hundred races and tongues. But the real exploration of the Sahara is comparatively recent. It was on September 22, 1826, that Major Laing,[1] the first martyr of the great desert, arrived at Timbuktu, the mystery city of Africa. A few days after reaching this Farthest South of the Sahara, he met a foul death at the strangling hands of his own treacherous escort.

A decade later, in 1836, another intrepid Englishman, Davidson, dared the vast unknown, to die after a heroic fight alone amid the dreaded sand dunes of Iguidi. His failure, and his tragic death, did not discourage his countrymen, for in 1845 the heroic James Richardson left Tripoli to cross the windswept sand barrens to the Sudan.

---

1. Major Laing's notes were destroyed by his murderers, and only a small portion of them were later found, buried in the sand. Again the desert reclaimed its own.

Then followed the important explorations of the Germans; Barth,[1] in 1855, and Rohlfs,[2] in 1867-69, and of the Frenchman, Duveyrier.[3] Their findings were the wonder of the world a scant three-quarters of a century ago.

For the explorer, the Sahara teems with interest and possibilities – lost oases, the rich emerald mines of the Garamantians (famous in old Rome), the treasures of Jupiter-Ammon, the alluring secrets of the "People of the Veil." I look back on happily glorious Saharan nights when, sitting in the lee of some sand dune, I have heard legends from the Arab, Siwan and Tuareg chiefs of buried treasure, lost oases, and of tombs guarded by the Djinns – evil spirits of the desert. And the treasures, the lost cities, and the great tombs really are there! I have seen them in the crystal dawn of the desert morn, a mirage that has become a realization, a legend that has become fact!

Whatever the explorer's scientific objective, he always will be impressed by the fascinating loveliness and the silent loneliness of the desert; he is certain to be enthralled by the mirage-like beauty of the oases and the mystery of the immense spaces, haunted by the ghosts of civilization that has vanished. Perhaps the sum of all these enchantments offers the reason why I, among others, have been drawn to make a life-study of the mystic land of gold and sand and ruin.

Duveyrier, the intrepid French explorer, who came into contact with the Tuareg and made the first scientific report on these "Knights of the Desert," as he called them, has remained the shining example and model of how an explorer should make an expedition and report faithfully his personal experiences, observations and scientific data. He belonged to that group of heroic pioneer explorers whose names are forever linked up with Mungo Park, who was drowned in

---

1. *Travels and Discoveries in North and Central Africa*, 6 vols., H. Barth.
2. *Quer dutch Africa*, G. Rohlfs.
3. See *Le Tuareg du Nord*, 2 vols., Paris, 1864, H. Duveyrier.

1805, in the rapids of Boussa, and with the names of Stanley and Livingstone, and with those other heroes of African exploration, Barth, Nachtigal, Pere de Foucauld, and that courageous officer, General Laperrine.

Young Duveyrier (19 years old) traveled lightly – a few camels, two servants and his scientific instruments made up his impedimenta. Simplicity and directness were keynotes of his nature and of his work. He traveled as the bold Tuareg tribesmen travel. No newspaper syndicate heralded his expedition or broadcast his every movement; there were no motion picture contracts to be had in 1860; no swift motor cars to eat up the interminable distances. He went alone, unguarded, without comforts, and despite the fact that this was rashness, to me he was a real explorer, an indomitable pioneer. The scientific results he obtained were as important as the net results of the modern expedition costing half a million dollars!

England, Germany and France were, during this period, the chief investigators of the Sahara. The English dead include Warrington, who died at Dibbela, south of Bilma. He was the companion of the German, Dr. Vogel. Dr. Oudney and Tyrwhit died in 1824 on the famous Clapperton and Denham expeditions. The brave Major Laing has been already mentioned. The explorer Richardson died south of Zinder in 1851, and his assistant, Corporal MacGuire, was murdered by the Tuareg. The heroic Ritchie died at Mourzouk in 1819. Clapperton lost his life at Sokoto in 1827; Davidson in 1836.

The German list of Saharan heroes is little known, but must be headed by that thorough and valiant explorer and scientist, H. Barth. Von Bary, Dr. Vogel and Overweg rest in graves in the Sahara that mark somber milestones in the history and exploration of that wide waste. The most notable Germans after these were Nachtigal, Hornemann, Schweinfurth, Rohlfs, Steindorf and Lenz. These men, by the imperishable records of their deeds, have inscribed their names in the golden annals of Saharan research.

To France belongs the longest list of Saharan martyrs. Last year was celebrated the hundredth anniversary of R. Caillie, who entered Timbuktu in 1828. He died on arriving in France, from exhaustion, incident to his terrible privations. He was only twenty-eight, but what high endeavor was crowded into those brief, swift years!

It is impossible to give the names of all those whose life blood has been drunk by the thirsty Sahara. I have seen the spots at Gurara where Lieutenant Palat was murdered in 1886, and where Colonel Flatters fell with ninety men at the dreadful Tuareg massacre of Bit Garama in 1881. I have visited the place where the Marquis de Mores died on the road to Ghadames in 1904. The tomb of brave Camille Douls, (1887) lies in a lonely, forgotten spot in the Tidikelt. Colonel Bonnier and his column were massacred by the Tuareg at Takorav in 1893. Joubert and Dournau-Dupere were assassinated near Ghadames in 1874. Then follow such names as Largeau; Father Bouchard and his missionaries, Fathers Richard, Pouplard, and Morat; Captain Martin, who died of thirst in the dunes of Iguidi; Lieutenant Leteyre; my friend Lieutenant Estienne, who died when I was in the Sahara; Father de Foucauld, who was foully murdered by the Tuareg at Tamanrasset in 1916; Coppolani, killed in Mauretania; General Laperrine, who perished south of the Hoggar in 1919, while attempting the first flight across the Sahara; and my good friends, General Clavery, Captain Debenne, Captain Pasquet, and Captain Resset, butchered as I write these words! Oh, but the list is endless! The Sahara has ever taken its toll without respect to race, to creed, to purpose, or to qualifications, but certainly France has her full quota of Saharan graves marked by the brief but forceful legend, *"Mort Pour la France."* Such is the price of exploration!

The most notable French explorers of the Sahara after Caillie and Duveyrier were de Foucauld, Gautier, Chudeau, Tilho, Cortier, Forneau, Lamy and Laperrine.

The massacre of Colonel Flatters and his expedition, in 1881, had such a paralyzing effect on Saharan exploration that it greatly retarded the work until the Tuareg defeat at Tit in 1902. To-night, around desert camp fires, hardy explorers still talk of that mysterious disaster which overtook Colonel Flatters and which equalled in horror the worst episodes in fatal expedition tragedies. I have heard, often, the ugly rumor that Colonel Flatters sought death in the Sahara, but it is inconceivable that such an explorer would lead ninety men to their death amidst the dreaded, merciless Tuareg.

The circumstances of the disaster were vividly described to the French Geographical Society by Duveyrier. I have stood at the spot, now marked by a monument at Ouargla, where the expedition collected and departed on its final and fateful trek. They were ambushed in the desolate, lonely valley in Tin Tarabin while watering their camels. Unquestionably they were betrayed by their Tuareg guides. Colonel Flatters and Captain Masson were the first to fall, as they had been separated from the main body. Captain Dianous, with the remainder of the column, then made his ghastly retreat northward. He tried to reach the wells of Amjid and his line of re-treat was a *Via Doloroso*. Their Tuareg guides, thwarted in their plans for wholesale murder, fed the remnant of the expedition with dates poisoned by the horrible Falazlez plant. This poison has a most startling effect. In some manner it upsets the victim's mental balance. Those members of the expedition who had eaten the poisoned dates became hysterical with laughter and were cut down by the jackal Tuareg as they ran into the desert. They died in the grim madness of raucous, mirthless laughter! The expedition suffered intensely. At last the food gave out, and then, in their distress and madness, they practiced cannibalism. When the harassed survivors reached the dreamed-of, longed-for wells of Amjid, they found the murderous Tuareg awaiting them and it is said that the haggard, worn wretches begged for a drink before dying. But the Tuareg is not a creature of mercy and this piteous request was denied the last survivors of this ill-fated caravan. Truly the Tuareg is "Forgotten of God."[1]

For many years it was rumored that several of the officers of this expedition had been captured by the Tuareg and held as slaves in the fastnesses of the Hoggar Mountains. There are several booklets and legends to this effect, but up to the present we have nothing to prove that any escaped the massacre save one Algerian soldier who, somehow, reached the north. I remember following a part of the route taken by this expedition in their desperate effort to reach the north, and have often pictured in my mind this most dreadful of all Saharan tragedies.

This disaster of Bir Garama remained unavenged until the famous battle of Tit, in 1902, when Lieutenant Cottonest killed a hundred Tuareg nobles and avenged Flatters. I heard the description of this battle from an eyewitness and saw the battlefield where the flower of the Tuareg nobles, armed with ancient flintlocks, mediaeval swords and shields, fell while attacking French machine guns. Although they were wiped out, this battle proved to all doubting minds the quenchless fires of valor burning in the hearts of these fearless and heroic desert people, who fought on when riddled with bullets, surrendering to death only when their bodies were literally cut to pieces.

Since that defeat the Tuareg has given up using the *"armes blanche"* – the crusader-like sword, shield and dagger of his ancestors. For centuries he had considered the gun as a weapon to be used only by the cowardly. The brave man, reasoned the Tuareg, would not be afraid to test his skill in a hand-to-hand encounter. That was a sporting prop-

---

1.   P. Vuillot, *Exploration Du Sahara*, Paris, 1895.

osition; but the gun, dealing death at great distances – well, to his mind, it simply wasn't cricket!

But he is a creature capable of adjustment, else he would not be a dweller in the Sahara, and the battle of Tit convinced him that to fight the devil (his simile, not the author's) he must use fire. To-day he is better armed than in past years, although he still continues rugged tournaments wherein the adversaries, armed like medieval knights, meet in the presence of noble ladies gathered to witness the jousting, and there wage battle with sword and shield. Or, mounted on horseback and armed with lances, they dash forward, royally armed for the joust.

One of the epic battles in the Sahara was the fight made by the Marquis de Mores, on the ancient caravan route from Carthage to Ghadames. De Mores made the fatal mistake of broadcasting to the people of the Sahara his intention of crossing the desert to open up trade with the Soudan. News is as swift as Mercury in the desert. It travels on the wings of the wind. In fact, it is uncanny how an event of no considerable importance often is reported hundreds of miles away. Before de Mores had progressed a hundred miles, with his richly outfitted caravan, the Tuareg were on his trail. For their place of attack they chose the desert waste near the well of Bir Ouiti. De Mores' caravan attendants were slain at the beginning of the attack. De Mores, though badly wounded, sought cover behind one of the small bushes so common in the desert reaches, and for three days and nights this gallant adventurer, single-handed, fought off the Tuareg with a murderous, unerring rifle fire unequalled in the most fanciful tales of desert fighting.

The Tuareg is not afraid to charge, and it must be that they did charge again and again. But de Mores was in the position of one who cannot afford to miss and he kept up a repelling fire with his rifle until the ammunition for that piece was exhausted. Then he was forced to use his revolver. Now, of course, the end was in sight. The last cartridge was used upon himself, cheating, in this last act, the blood-thirsty Tuareg. When his body was found, it bore sixteen bullet wounds. The hundreds of cartridges found near the bush bore witness to his heroic fight against fearful odds.

Several of his murderers were captured, due to their stupidity in trying to sell part of de Mores' baggage at Gabes and Tunis. From them we know the details of this lone Horatio of the Sahara. The spot where he fell was first marked by a stone monument, but in some mysterious way the memorial disappeared year after year. At last, the Topographical Service of the French army erected a monument of cement and stone at the top of a mountain looking down on the lonely plain and the battle spot of de Mores' death. But I have since heard that it has again been overthrown and, beyond doubt, this has been done by the Tuareg, who cannot forget or forgive the valiant last stand of a single man who held them at bay and died even more bravely than they know how to die.

Ever so often clews to some desert murder appear in the different markets of northern Africa – a gun here, a cloth cap there, and I, myself, have had the fortune to find Pere de Foucauld's handwriting in the ruins of his *bordj* at Tamanrasset, as well as to have obtained a relic of the Flatters disaster. I have also several relics from the battle of Tit, the saddle of King Moussa-Ag-Amastan, a map of the Hoggar by General Laperrine, and a score of other precious personal relics of Saharan explorers.

The Last Great Martyr of the Sahara

Pere de Foucauld,[1] "The Hermit of the Sahara," as he was called, is one of the most outstanding of all the great explorer-soldiers of the vast kingdom of sand. He was born of a noble French family and entered a military college at St.

---

1. *Life of Charles de Foucauld*, Bazin, R.

Cyr at the same time as his friend, General Laperrine. His military life was tempestuous, reckless and extravagant, but like the great St. Augustine of Carthage, he mended his ways and became a Trappist monk. In 1883-4, disguised as a Jew, he explored a considerable portion of the unknown Morocco. At Beni-Abbes he lived the life of a Trappist in a small half-cell, half-chapel that is one of the sacred spots in the Sahara to-day. During this time, slowly but surely, legends were growing up around this extraordinary man. He would walk hundreds of miles to succor the sick and destitute; his was a life of utter privation and suffering. His lofty ideals, humble spirit and goodness slowly endeared him to the hearts of the desert nomads. Finally he established himself in the very heart of the Sahara, in the midst of the wild Hoggar Mountains, and here, among the savage Tuareg, he built a hermitage. For many years, like the Anchorites of old, he dwelt alone in the desert, befriending all and trying to show the path of righteousness to the veiled ones – the Forgotten of God. I have seen the ruins of his hermitage at Beni-Abbes, and the one on the mountain top near Mt. Illiman, and at Tamanrasset, the capital of the Hoggar, where his final resting place has become a shrine.

His cell was no more than seven feet in length and five in width, but in each hermitage-chapel he built an altar for his hours of fasting and penitence, and it is interesting to note that the Pope had given him a special dispensation to hold mass alone. His self-inflicted privations were incredible; his food was less than the scanty Tuareg fare, and it must be that he suffered from the bitter cold of the nights as he lay stretched on the cold rock or sand floors of his pathetically small shelters. In summer he retired to his mud hermitage on the summit of a desolate mountain where, when in want of water, he was forced to descend a steep and rugged trail of over a thousand feet. Not infrequently illness came upon him here, but the Tuareg, who had learned to admire him, would climb to his aerie, fearing that the holy man, the white *marabout* (saint), had died in the midst of his solitude.

It is said that at one time he hovered between life and death for many days, – the result of an unfortunate encounter with a scorpion – until a military doctor could reach him from the outpost of Fort Motylinski. He used to accompany General Laperrine, his former military schoolmate, on the General's long expeditions to tame the desert folk. French officers still recount the amazing spectacle of General Laperrine on his camel being followed by Pere de Foucauld, who traveled on foot, bareheaded, holding to the tail of the General's camel, or trudging along far behind, battling the sand with the strength of his own weary feet. This was a part of his daily, self-inflicted penance.

His influence in the Sahara was great indeed. It was especially felt at the time of the World War and the subsequent Tuareg-Sinussi revolt which caused blood to flow in every part of the Sahara.

At the outbreak of the war de Foucauld's military training and love for his native land stirred his hermit heart to action. His chapel became a fortress and he the French Intelligence Department of the Sahara. His influence held the majority of the Hoggar Tuareg on the side of France, and soon he was such a force that the anti-allies plotted his death. From the far-away Fezzan the dark raiders came out of the night – the last saint of Africa was called to the door of his fortress-hermitage (which he opened, thinking it was the military post from Fort Motylinski) and the Judas act was once again enacted.

Pere de Foucauld was seized, his hands bound behind his back, and a single shot was fired. This shot, entering the neck, ranged downward and the holy man sank slowly to his knees, dying in the attitude of prayer. His three faithful servitors were killed a moment later and the assassins then made haste to cover up the evidences of their crime. They buried de Foucauld in the position in which he had fallen, in a pit in front of his chapel door. Near by, in a second hole, were thrown the three servitors who had long been with him. The hermitage was ransacked; the vessels of his chapel were overthrown; his monumental manuscripts of Tuareg lore, language and history were destroyed. The raiders disappeared into the night and he, who was known as "The Friend of All the Desert," joined the long list of Saharan martyrs who have given their lives in the establishment of great ideals.

Pere de Foucauld often had said that his purpose was to give his life to the holiest of causes, and while the long-forgotten spirit of the early Christians was truly in the heart of this last of that noble army, it is doubtful whether he would have willed it in just this fashion, for certainly his work was not yet finished.

For years he lay in an unmarked grave until that fateful day when another tragedy fell across the Sahara, and the body of the heroic General Laperrine was brought to be placed by the side of his life-long friend in a lonely sepulcher in the heartless, pitiless desert.

General Laperrine, styled the conqueror of the Sahara and France's greatest colonial soldier, died in the first military attempt to fly the Sahara. His plane came down, lost in the dreaded Tanezrouft, "The Land of Fear," and the General was injured in the landing. For two weeks he suffered torture from his pierced lung. Hunger and the pangs of thirst were slowly devouring him and his two companions. His companions had been unhurt in the landing, but their situation seemed hopeless – a little water from the radiator, a few bars of chocolate, and the scorching desert on every side.

General Laperrine's fortitude was Spartan-like. He knew he was dying. Time after time he tried to "cheat" himself out of his share of the water and chocolate so that his unwounded companions might last longer than he and thereby have a better chance of being rescued. The pathetic, yet inspiring circumstances of his death rank side by side with that of the heroic Oates, of Scott's last sad expedition.

Oates was that brave soul who, knowing that he was too exhausted to go on and was, consequently, an impediment to the safety of the rest of the expedition, walked bravely out into the blizzard of the Antarctic night where, alone, he met and embraced death. His grave is in the bleak wastes of the far Antarctic, marked with the glorious line: "Here lies a very gallant gentleman." What a striking epitaph! And surely I took nothing from the fame of Oates when, standing beside the seldom visited grave of General Laperrine, there came to me the words, "Here lies a very gallant gentleman."

The General's last words to his heartbroken companions were, *"Mes enfants,* if you are saved, tell all that I died thinking I knew the Sahara, but it was not so. In thirty years I have traversed the great desert only to die here, lost in a land I loved so well. Remember the Sahara is still the Sahara! It will always remain so."

Sorrow and consternation reigned from one end of the Sahara to the other as the news spread that the explorer-soldier was lost. Patrol after patrol of the General's own heroic desert "Goumiers" suffered thirst and exhaustion in their frantic search for their beloved leader. A lucky troop at last sighted the plane, upside down in the dunes. The pilot and mechanic were saved, but the General was dead. Only a mound of sand, on which had been reverently placed the General's red and gold "kepi," marked the preliminary resting place of this soldier of France. Later he was to make his last voyage to Tamanrasset, to be placed by the side of his martyred friend, Viscount Charles de Foucauld.

But a strange thing was recorded when Pere de Foucauld's body was removed to its new grave – a story to which I give full credit since it was told me by a reliable eyewitness of the ceremony. The hermit's body was found in the position in which he had died – his arms still bound behind his back, and he was on his knees in his grave in the attitude of prayer. The amazing fact is that his body had become mummified! Only the skeletons of the three servitors who died with him were found in their grave, but the martyr hermit appeared as he had so often been seen alive, and it is said that the effect of this miraculous circumstance was eloquent to the officers, soldiers, and Tuareg tribesmen present.

We might well name the spot where these two heroes lie buried "The Pantheon of the Sahara." This second burial ground of the noble martyred man of God and the great-hearted General Laperrine will remain forever symbols of all that is realistic and soul inspiring. A people who can give birth to such examples of human lives and endeavors have a right to empire, and we can have confidence in a work that is nurtured on the ideals and sacrifices of such heroic spirits as these two men, who now lie in eternal peace amidst the shadows of the Saharan mountains, blissfully unaware of the march of years, of shifting sands, or of the high endeavors of their followers who, inspired by their actions, follow the danger trail in the interests of science, progress and civilization.

Chapter 2

CAVE-DWELLERS OF THE DESERT

"There a temple in ruin stands
Fashioned by long forgotten hands;
Two or three columns, and many a stone
Marble and granite, with grass o'ergrown!"

– Lord Byron.

"Out of Africa, always something *new,*" runs an old saying. Since the days of that renowned reporter of ancient history, Herodotus, every year brings us new facts of interest
from out the still unknown reaches of the Dark Continent. I
remember reading, in school days, Herodotus' descriptions
of ancient Africa, and was particularly interested in his
accounts of the "Isle of the Lotus Eaters," and the land of the
Troglodytes, or cave-dwellers, on the far-off coast of the legendary Syrtian seas.

Our first expedition to these mountains and desert coun-
tries was in 1920, using Carthage[1] as our headquarters.
From that point we motored down the coast several hundred
miles to the land of the cave-dwellers. It is a weird region,
where fifty thousand human beings live like moles far under
the ground and have so lived since prehistoric times. It is
part of ancient Libya, a land known from the earliest legends
of antiquity, and from whence some of the strangest peoples

---

1.   It is not easy to dismiss Carthage with a word, but volumes could be (and have
been) written on this interesting field of exploration. See *Digging for Lost African Gods*, de
Prorok, *The Narrative Press,* 2001.

of the earth have issued. The home of these people lies under the towering Matmata Mountain range, which by mighty effort lifts itself above the Sahara and stretches southward in endless wastes of sand and sun-scorched plateaus.

It is difficult to reach this region in motor cars. The trails are rough and the dwellings of the Troglodytes often are perched in seemingly inaccessible, eagle-like aeries. Three times I have led scientists and students into the desolation of southern Tunisia in search of these prehistoric people, who have come down unchanged unto this day. On one of these trips we got as far as the forbidden city of Ghadames, and ourselves lived in caves, much like the Troglodytes.

One of our objectives was to excavate for prehistoric remains in the caves no longer used by the present day dwellers of that region. Our researches were crowned with success, for we brought back many thousands of worked flints, arrow heads, spearheads, and hatchets of the neolithic period.

The personnel of the expedition of which I now write was made up in the main of young men, with a few older men who were willing and physically fit to undertake the hardships of desert life. As in all expeditions, there were farewell parties, interviews by the press, the buying of equipment, and all the excitement and clamor incident to such preparation. At an early hour our caravan of cars left the Palais Hamilcar, which is built on the sight of ancient Carthage and serves as headquarters of the Franco-American Expedition to North Africa.

The sun was rising over the opalescent Gulf of Tunis as the motor cars wound their way through the groves of olive and cypress trees that cover the ruins of the cities of Dido and Hannibal. We were pointing south at last and, as usual, our moving picture operator filmed the departure. Poor Kellerman! He was always filming the departure or the arrival of the cars and, therefore, always was the last to leave and the first to take up his position at any important spot.

At Tunis a crowd gathered to see our cars get their last fill of gasoline, and to gaze in wonder at the human, begoggled, sun-helmeted golliwogs. There are few sensations more delightful than the realization of one's dreams. Always it is a supreme moment when a well equipped expedition finally gets under way, with all eyes turned toward great adventure.

The last car filled and we are off. The trail leads South, always South, and the cars follow the seacoast route along which heroes of antiquity once traveled by crude methods of transportation that were a far cry from the thundering motors of to-day. These same trails to the desert saw Hannibal and his mighty war elephants; they saw Cato and his foot-sore, defeated legion; they saw that mightiest of conquerors, Alexander the Great, crossing the burning sands to be proclaimed a god in a far-off oasis temple; they saw the victorious Scipio Africanus and the heroic Kahena, the Joan of Arc of North Africa.

Between Carthage and the Sahara one still uses the old trails of the Carthaginians and Romans, who spread their influence even into these wastes. World conquerors, they thought themselves to be, and though their influence is felt to this day, they did not conquer the Sahara, for along these old trails, which knew the tread of victorious armies, lie the unknown, sand-buried cities of a lost empire.

After three hundred miles of interesting travel, we at last approached the wild mountains of the Troglodytes, that rise out of the desert and frown down upon the old Syrtian gulfs, where lies the fabled "Isle of the Lotus Eaters."

The Djebel Matmata Mountains are a tumbled, jumbled mass of rocky pinnacles. Vegetation is scarce; only here and there are to be seen a few palm trees and patches of stunted grain. Desert travel is hard at best on automobile tires, but when one attempts to reach mountain aeries over a trail made up of sand, rock, and knife-like flints, then there is certain to be trouble with tires; every member of the expedition will earn his canned goods by the sweat of his brow.

On each of the three trips into this "devil region" we have had a different moving picture camera man, but the only one who came away from these mountains and was ready for more was Mr. Kellerman, of Pathe, brother of the world famous Annette Kellerman. The man seemed made of iron. Like a Trojan he climbed rocky fortresses, with heavy cases on his back. Perhaps his endurance may be accounted for by the fact that he could rid himself of his feelings in forceful and picturesque language. For centuries the great places around us had been silent, but a friend who returned recently from the Matmatas stoutly declared that the echoes of Kellerman's voice still are heard in the distant recesses of the mountains. I am quite certain that the Arabs hired by Kellerman are still resting from the exertions he forced upon them.

The camera man, on an expedition, is to be pitied. He must get pictures, and it is quite a problem to follow the activities of a group of archaeologists, geologists, prehistorians, press correspondents and botanists, all of whom are searching, digging, and scratching away in as many different places as they can possibly find. But Kellerman was nothing daunted, and I especially recall a scene where several members of the party were attempting to reach an inaccessible cave-dwelling by means of ropes attached to a pinnacle of rock above. The rocky ledge punished the knuckles and knees of the hardy explorers, yet Kellerman had the courage to shout to us to *"hold"* that scene so that he could "shoot" one of the members of the party dangling in the sky a full thousand feet above the floor of the Sahara. Kellerman got his picture, and the agony on George French's face as portrayed in the picture is anything but acting. It is interesting to note that this cave dwelling, which we reached by ropes, was used by the Troglodytes, and to this day we have not the slightest idea how they managed to reach the entrance.

The reader may wonder why the Troglodytes selected such inaccessible places for their residences. The choice was forced upon them; it was simply a matter of protection and race preservation. For hundreds of centuries the harassed Berbers have been raided by Carthaginians, Romans, Vandals and Tripolitan marauders in search of slaves. To escape capture, these unfortunate people sought refuge within caves on the dizzy pinnacles of rock.

We took up our own abode in one of these ancient caves. The rock floor upon which we made our thin bed was not conducive to long hours of sleep. But it was infinitely better than sleeping outside, where the biting cold winds of the mountain search one to the marrow. At first the entire party slept in the best cave to be found, closing the small entrance with a rug. Cosily situated, we looked forward to a good night's sleep. But alas! Our slumbers were disturbed by the representative of Oxford University, who would sleep on his back. He was one of the most sonorous and audible of sleepers. The raucous sounds which he emitted echoed through the neighboring caverns, and the volume of sound became doubly amplified. I thought for a moment that the mountain was volcanic. All members of the party awoke and promptly resolved themselves into a committee of the whole to sit in judgment upon the offender. He was unanimously voted out of the cave (his own vote being thrown out), and was forced to find another cavern with thick walls separating him from the rest of the expedition.

Only since the coming of the French, about fifty years ago, have the poor dwellers of this region had any peace. Their past history is a long and bloody page of massacre, raids, and the living death of being sold into slavery. In some of the rock aeries in the south Matmatas can be found poor human specimens who are scarcely more human than a jackal or a wolf. It is impossible to approach them. On one occasion one of our camera operators, the Prince de Waldeck, spent hours trying to get a snap-shot or a movie film of some of these wild people, but they disappeared in the rock fissures like so many timorous, panic-stricken rabbits.

The Digger Indians, and a tribe of northern Australian aborigines, are the only other people on the face of the earth so degraded as these people of the Matmatas. The French have done what they could, but it is a long and fruitless labor. Fear is their age-old heritage. They have no desire for civilization, and one may hazard the guess that their resistance to all efforts of civilization is based on the thought – if indeed they think – that if civilization is a matter of massacre, of raids, and of slave dealing, then they prefer to be uncivilized. Indeed, it is reasonable to suppose that the stag fleeing before yelping hounds and braying horns may have a slight opinion of the high-mindedness of man.

I remember the scene created at Kebir Matmata when an attempt was made by the French military doctors to halt a smallpox epidemic. These doctors made an attempt to vaccinate the women of the Matmatas, and a real battle ensued. Old rusty guns were brought out, knives were used, and the howling and cursing was beyond description. At last all of the men were made prisoners, but not until that moment could the women be overpowered and vaccinated. However, the end was not yet. The battle with the women was more hazardous than that with the men. Faces were scratched and handfuls of hair pulled out. One French officer, in his report to the Government, declared that only bald-headed doctors should be sent to the Matmatas.

The land is rife with superstitions and witchcraft, and while exploring the region around Bled Kebira, we had the good fortune to come across several medicine men. They performed weird dances that are almost identical in rhythm to the jazz of today. These medicine men are a distinct handicap to progress. They spread disease, expound fanatical ideas and advocate the most unsanitary practices. They claim that they come from some mysterious land in the heart of the Sahara. During their weird dances they utter high, screeching notes which remind one of the statement made by Herodotus, that the people who live in the bowels of the earth near the Syrtes, "had a cry like a bat, ran as fast as animals, and lived on snakes and lizards." So, in twenty-five centuries these people have not changed.

In the far south, the Troglodytes do not live in prehistoric caves. There they have built their villages underground and their dwellings are a series of dark rooms and a labyrinth of mole-like passages. It is extremely difficult to gain access to these underground haunts; difficult and dangerous, for the inhabitants are savage, their poverty is frightful, and their struggle for existence has given to their thin, wan faces a look of cruelty and suspicion. Now that peace has come at last to this land, it would be far better for them to come down from their mountain aeries to the plains, where life is easier. But they cannot forget the past.

The old men still remember the raids and fights of the early days with the pirates of Tripoli. Truly their eyes have beheld dreadful scenes of warfare that was not unlike the early frontier fighting with the Indians in America. There were swift and sudden attacks, which usually resulted in the massacre of the bolder, braver men, and the carrying off of the women into slavery.

In Roman times Sallust and Pliny spoke of the Matmatas as being covered with forests, but to-day the mountains are bare and desolate. It was into this region that the Carthaginians came to hunt and entrap their elephants. How strange to think that the huge wild elephants that once roamed the valleys and plateaus of this region were hunted and captured and trained in Carthage for warfare in foreign lands. When Hannibal crossed the Alps he had with him his elephants from the Matmatas. There, at least, they were at home in climbing the sky-limned passes.

What strange scenes must have been enacted when the Carthaginians were pursuing and trapping the elephants, which gained for them so many battles. That ingenious

Carthaginian who first thought of training these beasts and turning them into thundering instruments of war to beat the Romans, is equal to that Englishman who invented the tank and the effect upon the enemy was identical. New methods of frightfulness in warfare are not the property of any age. The Germans quailed before the onslaught of the Englishman's ironclad Juggernaut, and the Romans, armed with shields and short swords, fled panic-stricken before the ponderous war elephants of Hannibal.

It was in these same mountains that the Romans hunted the wild beasts for the gladiatorial shows at Carthage, Rome, El Diem, Utica, and other great cities of Africa. The amphitheatre of El Diem, the ancient Thysdrus, is halfway between the Matmata Mountains and Carthage. It is a monumental piece of architecture. Imagine a vast arena as large as the Colosseum of Rome, with a seating capacity of eighty thousand, suddenly rising before you out of the desert plains. We know nothing of its history. The traces of the ancient town are gone, and we can only gaze at the thousands of silent seats and wonder!

Such is this mysterious land of Africa! "Out of Africa, always something new." Rather, "Out of Africa, always something old," and so old and so mighty that the thoughtful man stands before it, feeling the force and wisdom of Job's mournful philosophy:

"Man that is born of woman is of few days, and full of trouble.
He cometh forth like a flower, and is cut down;
He fleeth also as a shadow, and continueth not."

During the months of our expedition to the south of Tunisia and Algeria, hardly a day passed without some new discovery or some unlooked-for adventure. The country has been well mapped by the French army, but it is so vast an area that there are many regions not yet fully explored. I remember passing through one of the plains between Gabes and the mountains, when far in the distance I saw a solitary pinnacle of rock. I turned my powerful glasses upon it, and it appeared there were dwellings on that pinnacle.

We promptly turned our cars in that direction, bent on investigation. It took us hours to reach it, but it was worth our efforts, both from a standpoint of topographical interest, as well as for the somewhat interesting, though not appreciated, adventure which befell us there. Rising abruptly out of the plain was a pinnacle of rock, not unlike the imaginary pictures of the Tower of Babel. On its summit was a cluster of houses, some of which were built of rock, while others were made of wood, mud and stones. There was not a sign of life and we concluded that the houses had been deserted.

After circling the mountain twice, and finding no pathway leading up, we decided to scale the nearly perpendicular face of the rock. For a while all went well. We had nearly reached the halfway limit when suddenly Pierre Geoffrey and Prince de Waldeck, who were in the lead, called: "Look out!" At that moment a small rock whizzed by my face.

In no uncertain language I shouted to my companions above to be more careful and not dislodge the rocks, else they might bring injury to some member of the party climbing after them. A suppressed yell was my answer as another rock missed Soubrier, a mechanic, by a hair's breadth. At this point I lost my temper, for that last stone would have killed Soubrier had it struck him.

I made an effort to join the party above and was calling them hard names when a small avalanche of sand and stones came down upon us from above. "What the devil!" Soubrier shouted as we watched the stones sweeping down the hill. We quickly placed ourselves under the lee of the rock to escape any further avalanche. Huddled there, we realized all too well that we were in error concerning the dwelling places being deserted. It was now painfully obvious that the

Troglodytes above were making use of prehistoric methods to keep us from getting up to have a look at them.

Prehistoric methods of warfare may be crude, but they are forceful. There was no alternative but to decamp, for it seemed hardly worth while to have our heads bashed in just to make a friendly visit to a Ksar, which was not more than sixty kilometers from the main road and, therefore, in what is supposed to be comparatively civilized country.

On the way down several more missiles went singing by, serving to increase our desire for the plain below. But when we reached it, we could see nothing moving on the heights above. We decided to inform the authorities at the nearest post, but our wrath was cooled somewhat by the fact that we had suffered only a few bruises, and by the consideration that the inhabitants of the rock city were quite within their rights, even though the method of preventing trespass was quaint and original. After all, they were only descendants of the Troglodytes, with hereditary hatred of strangers, and our uninvited friendly call had been but the prompting of curiosity.

The Troglodytes ever have been a hard people, if one is to believe Diodorus, Strabo, and other ancient historians. They killed the old men who were unable to follow the flocks; they gave names to the cattle who provided their substance but none to the family; they went naked, though the women wore a necklace of shells and amulets. Marriage was unknown and the female was far more important and more dangerous than the male. (Perhaps these two things are not peculiar to the Troglodytes!)

Their burial rites were unusual. The dead body, with legs and arms bound together, was set up on a mound and then with jeers and yells the cheerful Troglodytes pelted the dead body with stones. This is still the custom among these primitive people. After the body is literally covered with rocks and mutilated beyond recognition, a pair of horns is placed on the pile of stones and the crowd disperses with manifestations of great joy. There are many other details concerning the past and present practices of these people but they are too disgusting to find place in a work of this nature.[1]

Following our unpleasant adventure and flight from the pinnacled and mysterious Ksar, we journeyed southward of the Matmatas to another land of legends and phantoms. The Shotts, or inland lakes of southern Tunisia, are the legendary abode in whose foul depths dwelt the old sea monster, Triton, who, it will be remembered, once befriended Jason and the Argonauts. How strange it is that here in the desolate, dead region of the Sahara, the Greek legends of old still live to quicken the imagination with their beauty.

While exploring the rocks and caverns of the Matmatas that look down on the Shotts, we found traces of the Sun God, Ammon, sculptured centuries ago on the rocks and in the caves near these inland seas. From far-off Thebes and the Oasis of Jupiter-Ammon the cult of the Sun God had traveled into this distant region, and its followers had inscribed their faith on stones more lasting than their religion.

We have studied this cult in many parts of North Africa and have found traces of it in mystic symbols in the excavations at Carthage, Utica, Karanis and at the Oasis of Jupiter-Ammon. It must be borne in mind that some of these excavations are thousands of miles apart, separated by formidable mountain ranges and trackless wastes of sand, yet the cult of the Sun God hurdled all these natural barriers. It is strange, too, how the name of Alexander the Great spread to the remotest corners of the Sahara, after he had proclaimed himself a god at Siwa. Mountains and wells are still named after the great Macedonian conqueror and few other names have lived as long as that of Alexander.[2]

---

1. The modern day hill people of the Aures have customs that are unspeakable, which are derived, undoubtedly, from their ancestors, the Troglodytes. Even though these customs are revolting, it is interesting, nevertheless, to trace the survival of customs through the centuries.

2. See Chapter dealing with the Oasis of Jupiter-Ammon, where Alexander was proclaimed a god.

The region in which we now find ourselves is between the Matmatas and the billowing sea of sand called the Erg Oriental. It is one of the most fascinating parts of the Sahara, inhabited by a few half-savage nomads, with now and then a stray camel wandering among the dunes. The sand dunes in this region cover four or five hundred square miles.

It was while camping south of the dried-up inland lake of Djered that I saw for the first time those dreaded "People of the Veil," the Tuareg. Night was just coming down when a caravan of gigantic veiled figures, mounted on their great white Mehari camels, appeared suddenly out of the sand and passed us as silently as so many ghosts. They made no sound as they passed in the soft sand and their size seemed magnified by the flatness of the surrounding desert. Slowly, without a sign of greeting, and gazing straight ahead at the darkening horizon they disappeared into the night shadows, leaving behind a mental picture not soon to be forgotten.

How they would have enjoyed murdering us! We could feel their silent enmity as they passed the hated camp of a handful of Roumi. Needless to say, a strict guard was posted that night, for the Tuareg cannot always hold his hatred in hand. Every now and then the good old feeling comes back of the days when he was master of a country as large as the United States and was free to raid, steal, and massacre to his heart's content.

It is only recently that I lost one of my dearest friends, the brave Lieutenant Estienne, who was massacred with his party not far from the spot where we witnessed the silent passage of the Tuareg band. He was in one of my specially built, six-wheeled Renault desert cars, accompanied by a mechanic and three guards. Suddenly out of the sand came the dreaded, swift attack. It was over in a minute. The car was found a few days later with poor Estienne's body, which was terribly mutilated, as is the Tuareg custom. Empty cartridges gave proof of his brave defense. Around the wrecked car were the tracks of many camels – and another page was written in the voluminous history of mysterious and unexplained horrors of the Sahara. Estienne's murderers were never found, only a faint trail led into the wild, unknown region where no man dare follow.

The region around Gafsa and Negrine is often unsafe, despite the fact that military patrols are exceedingly vigilant. It is a big country, and it is impossible thoroughly to police it. Once, when camping in the desolate region near the ruins of the city of Ad Majores, we were taken for a party of murderers. The military patrol had seen our camp fire and, as we were off the beaten track, it was thought possible by the lieutenant in command that it was the camp of escaped bandits whom he was then pursuing. So silently were we surrounded that we knew nothing of what was going on until suddenly faced by a half dozen menacing guns. In the darkness we failed to recognize the men as the military mounted Meharists, and for a moment we thought our last hour had come. After giving us this fright, the officer regaled us for the remainder of the evening with desert tales of raids and pursuits. His supply of stories seemed endless, and it was well toward morning before we turned in for a few hours of sleep.

At the present moment of writing there is a body of bandits, quite famous locally, hiding in the canyons and hidden caves of the Matmata Mountains. While exploring the caves of this region the prehistoric writer, scholar, and scientist are often in danger. There is always an excellent chance for the explorer to find a few hidden murderers where he had hoped to dig up some flint – and of the two, the Matmata assassin is the harder specimen. It will take months to bring this band to bay, and then a real battle will ensue amid the rocky crags. There will be fighting from boulder to boulder, as is depicted in the best regulated Wild West film.

One of the most heroic annals of history took place with this very region as a stage; it was here that La Kahena, the valiant Berber Queen, made her last stand against the invading Arab hordes from the east. The mountain people of the Matmatas, Aures, and Atlas still talk of the mighty deeds of this Joan of Arc of Africa. She won battle after battle over the invading Arabs, but was finally crushed by overwhelming numbers.

Many of the battlefields still are pointed out, and the spot where the lion-hearted Queen was beheaded is sacred throughout North Africa. At the battle of the Matmata lowlands she defeated Hassan, Governor of Egypt, and killed forty thousand men. She rode a milk-white charger, was clad in armor, carried her white banner upon which was emblazoned the tribal emblem, and it is said that her six magnificent sons invariably rode at her side. She, herself, wielded a two-handed sword with all the spirit of warring fury. Her last stronghold was the colossal amphitheatre of El Diem, where for three years she remained undefeated. It was there she built the wonderful subterranean passage to the sea, which was twenty miles away, and this explains how she was able to bewilder the starving besiegers by throwing down from the battlements fresh fish to appease their hunger.

This, indeed, was magic, and earned for her the title: "The Witch of the Atlas." Despite her energy, skill and leadership, she at last was overwhelmed. Her name now stands beside such outstanding figures as Jugurtha and Koceila, and if we may link the past with the present, she well may take her place with that tenacious warrior, Abd-el-Krim, leader of the last of the Berbers, the brave and freedom loving Riffians.

Before reaching Kebili we visited the famous Neolithic sites at Ain Saiden, which were explored by the great German scientist, Schweinfurth. Here we found many links with the prehistoric evidences found in the Libyan Desert, and especially with those tiny flints called "pigmy flints" found in the Faiyum and at Siwa. They are so small that it is a puzzle to discover their purpose and uses. Though beautifully worked, they are sometimes as small as the finger nail and some of them less than half that size.

The region north of the half dried up Shotts of Jerid and Melghir is a veritable treasure region for the historian. For many weeks we explored the mountain ranges of Feriana, Gafsa, Seldja, Tebaga and Cherb. The desert canyons that lead from the mountains to the inland Saharan Shotts must have had a vast population in paleolithic times. In the region of Gafsa we visited the famous caves of El Mekta and the sites at Ain Guetar, Sidi Mansour, Bir Oum Ali, Ain Movlares, Redeyef and Tamerza.

There are few more wonderful views in this world than the gorges of Seldja, called by the Arabs "The Gateway of the Sahara" but which we called "The Valley of the Thousand Caves." A small stream passes through this gorgeous valley. Its waters are clear blue and green, while the towering canyon walls are of vivid blood-red rocks with here and there a touch of old gold shading off into dark amber. Small canyons find their way into the larger depression, creating purple and mauve gashes in the sun-painted walls of the magic valley.

Time after time, year after year, I have been fascinated by this unbelievably beautiful canyon, and though my palette and brush have attempted it a hundred times it is impossible to catch the riotous coloring. One spot is a great favorite of mine – a small shady platform of stone just opposite the majestic pinnacle rocks that form the gateway to the Sahara. The gateway to the Sahara! To me these are magic words. Here, always, I am seized by the lure of what lies beyond; the challenge of the unknown!

Beyond this gateway lies the desert – two thousand miles of romance and mystery, a land of dreadful sufferings, of cruelty, of dead history and time-forgotten people.

Though seeking the problems and secrets of the past and scientifically placing on record the result of our researches into the question of the dawn of man, one cannot put aside the beauty and poetry of the scenes that seem to pass in review. The spell and the gift of contemplation is given one, when touching the silences of the desert. The spirit begins to know peace. The mad frenzy of modern life is forgotten. Thought takes on more dignity, moves more searchingly and the thinker begins to hunger for the deeper grandeur more satisfying than things.

The gift of contemplation! It is the gift of power enabling one to ponder the problems of life and eternity as did the Greeks of old, and to forget the fever of modern life with its complications, anxieties, and for once escape the ghastly bondage of things! I, for one, am eternally rebellious against being held in thrall by things, and I find that rebellion nearer success in the desert than in any other place. There I have the silences, the lure of the horizon-bound sand, the romance of the golden ruins buried therein.

There old stones speak to me in a language of their own and bring to me a satisfaction infinitely deeper than I can find in the busy market places. If only I could give the message of beauty to those who can never know the desert peace; if only I could show the silent ruins that speak so eloquently of a golden age when man in pomp and glory thought only of the day and reckoned himself permanently established; if only I could show you the desert I could show you how temporal is man and all his hopes, and how lasting is beauty and art. . .

But I must cease my philosophizing and climb down from my rocky pinnacle above the gorges of Seldja and across the mountains to the valleys of Tebessa, where lie the remains of other past civilizations.

The trail from southern Tunisia to Algeria is off the beaten track and yet it is like some great open-air museum. There are hundreds of ruins in this Saharan border region. There is the vast Byzantine fortress, Kasserine, and to the north the lovely temples at Sbeitla. The trail from the gorges of Seldja to Tebessa reminds one of the Appian way near

Rome, for the dead are buried in countless mausoleums all along the way. Gafsa, the scene of many battles of the Jurgurtine war, Feriana, Sidi Aich, Kasserine and Sbeitla Thala are all skeleton remains of a once great population and of a productive, prosperous region.

Mr. Gsell, of the Institute, and Mr. Louis Bertrand, of the French Academy, were my first guides to African history, literature and archaeology, and I recall that while staying with Mr. Reygasse at Tebessa, Mr. Gsell told me that he had mapped three hundred ruins south of Tebessa alone.

South of Tebessa are to be found the second greatest prehistoric regions of North Africa. It is the domain of Professor Reygasse, who as the government administrator of the region has combined his official work with scientific researches. El Ma-el-Abiod, Saf Saf, and the Djebellana are some of his most important fields, and we spent many weeks visiting sites of ancient civilizations that date back three hundred thousand years B.C. Mr. Kellerman, our movie operator on the entire trip, was made to film thousands of flints, much to his consternation and amazement, and several times remarked, "My boss in New York will think I have gone nutty, taking up so many hundreds of feet of precious film on a lot of ugly looking stones."

This is the strange land of the "Escargottiers," the snail eaters of prehistoric days, and to this day there are mounds of snail shells and flints which sometimes reach a height of forty feet. For thousands of years these simple folk subsisted on snails as their chief article of food. Personally, I can enjoy a dozen snails now and then "a la Bourgeyne," but I should hate to face them as a steady diet.

However, in southern Florida and along the Atlantic seaboard, I have seen great mounds of oyster shells which may in some dim to-morrow prove quite amazing to the sophisticated explorer bent on uncovering the best and the worst about us. No one race of people can become dictators in the matters of taste. The Siwans eat earth (and I have been told, though I cannot vouch for the fact, that there are a few earth-eaters in the mountainous regions of Tennessee and Kentucky); the Tuareg find grasshoppers a great delicacy; we have filmed negroes of Temacine eating live scorpions; the Troglodytes eat snakes and lizards, and old Pliny spoke of the dog eaters of Southern Tunisia.

The Aures Mountains, southwest of the prehistoric sites of Southern Algeria, is another interesting region which has been deeply studied by Hilton Simpson.[1] The people dwelling in these wondrous mountains are pure Berbers. We investigated many of their strongholds built in the solid rock of forbidding precipices.

One of the rivers which we ascended in this region is one of the loveliest I have ever seen. Its source is several miles east of Biskra – Robert Hichens' "Garden of Allah" – and winds its way through a canyon whose sheer walls leave only a ribbon of blue to indicate the sky. As the waters glide down to the Sahara they pass over marble beds that reflect "that tent of blue which prisoners call the sky," and turn the clear waters into a stream of liquid turquoise.

The people who live in these mountains are a half-savage division of the great Berber stock, which is the human substratum of North African peoples. Kabyles, Shawias, the Shelloohs and Riffians of Morocco, the Troglodytes of the Matmatas, the fierce Tuareg, the puritanical Djerbians, and the far-off Siwans are all of the same origin and descendants of the Cro-Magnon of primitive man. They have never mixed with the invaders of Africa and have always fought fiercely against them. In defeat they have retired to the mountains or to the Sahara, and as a consequence have never advanced.

The brilliant empire of Carthage came and went but it left no imprint on the Berber. Egyptians, Phoenicians, Carthaginians, Romans, Byzantines, Vandals, Arabs and the

---

1. *Hill Folk of the Aures*, London.

French have passed through this historic land, and though they left behind them magnificent cities to be swallowed by the sand or to stand in lonely grandeur in some mountain pass, they found the North Berbers as unchanging as the desert itself.

The Berbers were always great soldiers. As allies of Hannibal they well-nigh conquered the world, and at other times they invaded both Spain and France. The Berbers have been scorned for having gained nothing from the Carthaginians, Greeks, and Romans, but to-day they are a hearty, enduring race and one can but wonder if this is not the result of their racial strength which refused to mix with the empire builders who are no more.

The last great Riffian war was made by the direct descendants of Hannibal's Numidian cavalry. They are of Queen Kahena's heroic Berbers and of the same blood as Massinissa of Jugurtha and Koceila. This same blood has produced a host of modern time heroes, including Abd-el-Kader and Abd-el-Krim. Yes, they are still a separate and distinct race. They are still fighting for the privilege of being let alone, while old Carthage and Byzantium are but history.

The Riffs have learned a few great lessons from the desert – the love of freedom, the love of the beautiful and simple things of life. I hazard the prediction that they will still be Berbers and still ruling the desert and the mountains of North Africa long after the present empires of England, France and America have passed away.

Strange old cults are still alive in these Saharan border lands, survivals of Totemism and of the Carthaginians' goddess, Tanit, who was of Libyan origin; the cult of Aphrodisium, whose ruins are still to be seen near Hammamet, south of Carthage; the cult of Aissaoua, those terribly fanatical Berbers who practice barbaric self-violations; strange death customs among the Tuareg; and unspeakable rites among the Siwans of to-day. All of these cults have come down through the ages in a race that has changed but little since prehistoric times.

I have been asked many times if we have ever found traces of Punic ancestors in the people of the desert. I once went into the desert to study an oasis south of El Oed, where dwelt a people quite distinct and different from their neighbors. It is possible that a Carthaginian colony sought refuge here after Scipio had wiped out the Phoenician empire in Africa. We found that their cranial measurements corresponded in detail with the skulls excavated in the Punic tombs at Carthage. Like the Carthaginians of old, the chief characteristic of the merchants of this ancient oasis was their great trading superiority over the Arabs and Berbers that surrounded them.

The Mozabites, who live in the region of Ghardaia, also seem to be a people entirely apart from the other North African races. They have many of the Phoenician characteristics – extraordinary genius for trading, the Semitic trait of keeping themselves and their belongings well within the confines of their domain. They are splendid colonists, town builders, and are fearless pioneers. These distinct people, living in a beautifully cultivated oasis, are probably the last remnants of the once mighty Punic empire. A deep study is here ready for some one and it has many highly interesting phases.

North Africa and the entire Sahara is still an open field of research. There are many people to be studied ethnographically, regions to be explored geographically, and there is a vast archaeological and anthropological field only recently discovered. The vast sites investigated by us in southern Morocco, in the Oed Draa, Ain Sefra, southern Oran, the regions of southern Algeria and Tunisia, as far as the Ahaggar,[1] to the Libyan Desert and across the Nubian desert, all prove that we have here the greatest expanse of paleolithic civilization in the world.

---

1.   Ahaggar is the Tuareg form of Hoggar; another example showing the musical values in their language.

For nearly ten years I have tried to interest the scientists of America in this practically virgin field, first discovered by de Morgan, P. Boudy, Capitan, and Professor Reygasse. The interest, however, has been more in the Asiatic expedition to the Gobi Desert in Mongolia, though no paleolithic human remains have been uncovered by these vast undertakings, while the contrary can be said of the new field for African exploration.

We are now planning an expedition to the unexplored region of Mauretania and the savage Rio Del Oro. The coast line that is Spanish territory is practically unknown and strangely enough is one of the most important fields with respect to the study of human origin. Geologists and zoologists are of the opinion that a great area of land disappeared beneath the sea off the coast of Mauretania and Rio Del Oro.

Although we have few facts concerning the Lost Atlantis, it is in this district that a serious study should be made of this highly engrossing question.

On our coming expedition our route will be south of the Atlas and along the coast line where the ancient historian, Ptolemy, spoke of a great Libyan-Berber people who gave name to the region now called the "Senegal." These mysterious Sanhadjas were veiled nomads of the great Berber Tuareg-Libyan stock. They were powerful people in the past and known in the Fourth Century as the Almoravides, who conquered Morocco and Spain. No other Saharan people have held such a place in history. Manuscripts speak of ancient cities, such as Sibgilmessa, where traces of this empire still are to be seen. On our coming expedition we hope to find the dead cities of the ancient Melano-Getulienes, mentioned by Herodotus and other historians. We also hope to find some of the semi-legendary tombs of the lost Zenagas, who dwelt in the mountains of Rio Del Oro. Our route will pass through the land where the dreaded Maurs now live. The ancestry of these people was the basic stock of the fierce Moors. Little is known of this land. We are hoping to make friends with the unconquered and savage Oulad, Delim and Reguibats, for friendship is the only passport that is worth a farthing in that country. No man knows what may be found in that region, for as Professor Gautier reminds us, "There is no region in all the Sahara, including the Libyan Desert, so little known as the mysterious Rio Del Oro."

Fortunately, it will not always remain unknown, for so long as the race of man endures there will be explorers, and an explorer simply cannot be at peace so long as there are unknown wastes to cross and new trails to be blazed.

Chapter 3

THE HOGGAR EXPEDITION

"'The world has made such comet-like advance
Lately in science, we may almost hope,
Before we die of sheer decay, to learn
Something about our infancy; when lived
That great, original, broad-eyed, sunken race
Whose knowledge, like the sea-sustaining rocks,
Hath formed the base of this world's fluctuous lore."

– Festius.

For years my ambition was to explore the mysterious realms of the Sahara, the legendary Hoggar, and visit the secluded home of the "People of the Veil."

Wonderful tales of ancient ruins, of treasure tombs and of the emerald mines of antiquity, had come to my ears for many years. I had heard of deep, unexplored canyons, where the "Forgotten of God," the fiery Tuareg, made their strongholds; and of the forbidden, haunted mountains in whose caves the treasures of the marauders were amassed. Then, too, there were tales of fighting and of massacre a bloody past, in which many an expedition had perished in efforts to add one more page of knowledge to the terrible history of the Sahara.

This wide and little explored land often has been connected by writers and historians with the legend of the Lost Atlantis. It is a lost world of itself, a mountain region larger than that covered by the Austrian, Italian and Swiss Alps, surrounded by thousands of miles of pitiless, sun-scorched desert.

Forbidding though the land is, and filled as it is with adventure and great hazard, there is about it, nevertheless, a great lure, and this lure finds its origin not only in the facts at our hands and in the legends, but in the stimulating and exciting hope of what is yet to be discovered.

It was due to such a fascinating prospect that I conceived and prepared the first archaeological expedition to the wild stronghold of the veiled Tuareg tribes. The real object of this expedition was to add something to our knowledge of the ancestors of these "People of the Veil," and to discover, if possible, something more concerning the legendary Queen Tin Hinan and perhaps bring back substance to replace legend. The name of Queen Tin Hinan has come down from antiquity, although the late romance of Pierre Benoit has given the name of Antinea to this great queen of the Hoggar.

Clearly the first thing to do in preparing for an expedition was to secure all available maps and documents on the region to be explored. What cannot be bought must be borrowed from the government or the geographical writers, and if all of these are not sufficiently comprehensive – and they rarely are – then the leader of the expedition must add a few guesses to his knowledge. Not infrequently the success of the expedition hinges upon the accuracy of his guesses. An explorer is never armed with the whole truth concerning the country into which he goes, and it is not uncommon for some of his largest finds to be the result of a "hunch."

Maps, both ancient and modern, have always had a great fascination for me. How many delightful hours are spent before starting an expedition, in poring over the maps of the region one is on the point of entering. I can remember many delightful evenings spent with members of an approaching expedition, all gathered around the large table, with the maps spread out before us. This scene is generally enacted in my "museum-den" at home with the relics and souvenirs of my earlier expeditions covering every inch of the walls. Then there are relics of the great explorers of the past – a compass from the ship of Captain Cook; a piece of one of Shackleton's sleds; the letters and signed photographs of Pere de Foucauld, Amundsen, Scott, and a score of others.

Such relics are not dust-covered mementoes hoarded by greedy collectors; they are vital things, animated, spirited, challenging the workers and students to higher endeavor. And further to whet our appetites, there are the objects of antiquity dug up in many an archaeological enterprise – gold earrings from a Punic tomb at Carthage; shell-encrusted amphores and vases from the submerged Phoenician city of Tipasa off the Isle of Djerba; bracelets from the tomb of some light-footed dancing girl of ancient Utica; a beautiful carved emerald necklace of precious stones from Cleopatra's sumptuous palace at Mersa Matru; coins bearing the classic profile of Alexander the Great from the Temple of Jupiter-Ammon in the heart of the Libyan Desert, and hundreds of prehistoric flints from all over the Sahara.

Some of these relics, dug from the sand by my own hands, have a compelling interest, such as the ivory combs and hairpins bearing the inscribed names of unknown beauties, dead these thirty centuries; toilet articles of a lady of culture from the once luxurious city of Utica; scissors, a bronze mirror, perfume vases; an incense burner; rouge and eyebrow pencils; and (let carping critics of the modern girl ponder this line) a real vanity case!

Yes, there is romance in these ancient and worn objects. Romance and pathos, and for the Carthaginian lady who used them so many centuries ago, we can but give the "tribute of a sigh."

Alongside these objects of feminine vanity and glory range the heavy, cruel weapons of many a lost civilization – flint knives and hatchets from the Hoggar; the swords and daggers of the Tuareg; a gladiator's helmet from the Circus of Carthage; a spearhead from one of Hannibal's battlefields; a bronze arrowhead from the ruined walls of the Acropolis of Siwa, and an obsidian knife from the temples of Tenochtitlan. On my walls these weapons range alongside the objects used for the beautification of the ladies of old, yet perhaps they are not quite out of place, for some student may yet offer proof that had ladies been less beautiful there would have been fewer arms and wars and rumors of war.

It is rather stimulating to sit there in the room, gazing at our maps and seeing through a haze of tobacco smoke the souvenirs of so many thrilling moments during the uncovering of a lost city or the exploring of some unknown land.

Perhaps we are digressing, and should come down to the hard facts, but the explorer is not an alien to romance and it is natural that he should have dreams of some day locating Cleopatra's or Hannibal's tomb, of finding traces of the Lost Atlantis, or of finding the "Lost Oasis." But the dreamer-explorer cannot keep his head in the clouds. He must come down to the hard, stern, exacting business of organization.

To organize an expedition into the Sahara there are endless preparations in store – the raising of great sums; the procuring of government permits and collaboration; the testing of the specially made desert-car-tanks; the establishment of depots of gas, water, food and ammunition in properly placed stations across the desert; the purchase of scientific instruments, such as tents, pickaxes, guns, moving picture cameras, films, wireless, and specially made boxes for antiquities; hundreds of presents for the natives; military protection, and a thousand and one things that seem to make the great moment of departure years away. I believe that the worries incident to the preparation of an expedition are harder to bear than the labor and hardships in the actual exploration and excavation.

The responsibility is another great charge, especially when you are leading a party of men into distant and unknown regions. And the Sahara, despite the military outpost, the wireless, the aeroplane, the automobile, is still the same unconquerable desert, where disaster is certain to overtake the unprepared and unwary. It is remarkable, too, how easily one can get lost in the Sahara. My own personal experiences there offer examples of how one can stray from the caravan and get lost,[1] when as a matter of fact one is only a few hundred yards from camp.

Near Ouargla, a few years ago, two French soldiers strayed a little way from their caravan. The desert swallowed them. Madness overtook them within twenty-four hours and their bodies were found only eight miles from the town of Ouargla. Eight miles can be a thousand leagues in the Sahara. I have before me a recent newspaper clipping, giving an account of a party being lost in the region near the Pyramids! Death and the Sahara are age old allies.

Time, even for the restless explorer, passes at last and the days of preparation are at an end. The hour of departure is at hand. The cars are ready and we go through the last exciting moments known to all who are about to leave for the unknown. There are preliminaries, the next to the last and the last farewells with loved ones, the clasping of hands with friends and well-wishers. the waving of the hand, the cheering and Africa lies before us!

The voyage to Algiers may be here disregarded in the same way it was disregarded by all members of the party. All eyes are toward the Sahara and there is no excitement in a short sea voyage. Days spent on board ship are laggard days, for we are anxious to set our three giant twelve-wheeled Renaults on African soil. Even old Algiers, Constantine, Biskra and Touggourt are to the purposes of this expedition but points on the map which must be reached and passed before we come to the place where nothing lies before us but a few oases which spot the "endless span of the great desert."

---

1. See Chapter 6.

When we reached the last spurs of the Aures Mountains that look over the sea of sand, we climbed out of the cars and drank to our success as we gazed across the far horizon that came to rest in the land of gold, of sand, and of ruins.

As we came down from the mountains an extraordinary and unforeseen adventure overtook the party. The three cars were following the rough trail that led to Touggourt when suddenly the leading twelve-wheel Renault slipped down an embankment and into a swiftly running river! There had been a cloudburst the night before and the whole of this section of the Sahara was flooded. Our three powerful cars were made for desert travel, for sand dunes, rocks and mountains, but were absolutely unprepared and unfitted to go through mud! They had been so constructed as to carry drinking water and gasoline for at least eight hundred kilometers at a stretch. Each car weighed over four tons and was loaded with guns, powerful flashlights, camping equipment for a dozen men, pickaxes, moving picture camera, boxes of films, many spare tires and cases filled with tinned foods. In all, the weight was very considerable.

I shall never forget the triumphant procession of the giant cars down the Champs Elysées, with the French and American flags on each motor, looking not unlike three great tanks, especially since on one of them was mounted the modern death-dealing tool of Mars a machine gun. That had been a glorious start, but now one of the cars, which we had nicknamed "Lucky Strike," was ingloriously stuck in the mud of that rarest of rare things – a Saharan flood!

One of the cars was fitted with a cable spool attached to the motor shafting, a device designed for pulling cars out of the sand. We tried to utilize this cable on poor "Lucky Strike" but the mud was too deep. The river was rising rapidly, and for the moment it seemed that we were going to lose one car and possibly some lives at the very outset of the expedition. What a headline that would have made for a newspaper syndicate more interested in glamorous reports than in scientific data. Drowned in the Sahara! That is what a newspaper man would call news! But the papers were spared this recital due to the difficulty being solved by the hiring of an entire Arab village which our guide, Chapuis, knew of some three or four miles away. Fortunately the cars were fitted with strong ropes for the mountain climbing, which we knew was in store for us once we reached the hill region, and with some thirty Arabs pulling and twenty pushing, and with the members of the expedition pushing the Arabs, we managed to drag the heavy cars through the ever thickening mud and water.

Our camera man, with a nose for news as well as an eye to drama and footage, shot many feet of this unusual scene, showing the motor cars lurching and plunging through water and mud. No little amusement was caused when one of the ropes gave way and a score of Arabs landed flat on their faces in the mud and water. This native man-power was obliged to stay with us until we had worked the cars up to the drier highlands.

To the northeast of Biskra, not far from the area where the flood took place, the famous "Mountain of Snakes" lifts its towering pinnacles of rock above the desert. It is certainly one of the strangest of sights, for the mountain is literally honeycombed with thousands of holes made use of by the dreaded nadjda, the cobra of Africa. The mountain, it is said, has been used since early antiquity as a salt quarry and this accounts for the many corridors and snake infested pits. In the evening the snakes come out of their dens by the hundreds and the mountain is fairly writhing with poisonous reptiles which attack on the slightest provocation.

"The Cursed Site," as the Arabs call it, has witnessed many tragedies. The natives told us that until quite recently the nadjda was used as a hideous instrument of revenge, the favorite mode of procedure being to leave one of these snakes in the home of the intended victim. It is known that prisoners of the fighting tribes were brought here to die in some loathsome cavern of the mountains.

On the walls of many of the metal and salt mines of this region we have found the names and prayers of early Christian slaves and martyrs. Thousands of slaves perished here during the early Christian persecutions and the dreadful work in the salt mines. Some of the inscriptions found here are heartbreaking in their appeal for liberty or death, and it is said that hundreds of these slaves were kept in the bowels of the earth and never more saw the sun. Louis Bertrand, the great French academicien and novelist, has told in his books the tale of their sufferings, especially in that masterpiece, "Sanguis Martyrum" (Blood of the Martyrs). This great novelist found a wonderful field for his vivid expression, as Africa was at one time the great center of Christian scholarship and doctrines.

In North Africa one ever feels the spirit of the old Fathers, and the great chain of their basilicae stretches from Morocco to Tripoli, a mighty testament to the strength of the early Christians in this far land. St. Augustine, St. Cyprian of Carthage, St. Perpetua and St. Monica are among the great martyrs of the Church who died for the Faith in this savage land.

Leaving this region, which provided such a tragic page in the efforts to Christianize Africa, we move on in a southwesterly direction. Night has fallen and we are feeling our way across the desert, lighting up the faint trail with our powerful flashlights. On the left we begin to see the dim outline of the great dunes of the world's largest sea of sand the awful Erg Oriental, which covers a vast area and whose deeps contain unexplored problems. At night, under the moonlight, these dunes give one the impression of a stormy sea suddenly arrested in its wild turbulence and molded into silent, monstrous waves of sand. "Don't leave the trail," the Arabs say here, "for who wanders to the east goes immediately to the devil."

Suddenly out of the night we saw the lights of Touggourt. In the distance the lights seemed a continuance of the
firmament of stars overhead and showed with crystalline
intensity in the clear air of the Saharan night. As we slowly
wound our way through the labyrinth of bushes and desert
shrubs that surround the ancient city, we passed the great
tombs of the desert kings of Touggourt. The impression created in the pale African moonlight was weird indeed. The
white domes, with their little black windows and doors,
resembled a group of enormous skulls lying in the sand.

We stopped for a moment to visit the silent sepulchre.
The tombs of the Marabout are shelters in the desert, and so
made as to offer refuge in case of sand storm or nocturnal
attack. The tomb of the saint is placed in the center and in
the midst of the many offerings from pilgrims, and a half-
ruined staircase leads up to a small room in the tomb where
pilgrims and others rest and pray.

I recall a sacrilegious practical joke played by a young
American student on some innocent Arab workmen who
were using one of the tombs as a shelter at night. This ingenious young joker took a long rubber tube, buried it under
the sand and then placed one end in the tomb. Following
that, in all seriousness, he made the statement that he felt
certain the tomb was haunted and asked us to watch it at
midnight. We made ourselves comfortable around the camp
fire in the lee of the sand dune, where we could see the white
dome of the sacred tomb rising above the surrounding
desert. Suddenly we heard the most unbelievable commo-
tion issuing from the edifice. A score of Arabs hastily
emerged, and to make sure their escape began tearing across
the desert at a mad pace. All the while the weirdest of wails
were issuing from the usually silent tomb.

The young American was particularly pleased by his
inventive turn of mind. The unearthly sounds which he had
uttered through the tube had served to convince the Arabs
that the dead of past centuries had most certainly returned to

mock them. Their precipitous exit was all that the American could have hoped for. Of course, it was somewhat amusing to see the white-robed Arabs jabbering and quaking and racing for the dunes, but even the superstitious Arab is entitled to the peace of his slumbers, and I considered it a joke deserving no special commendation.

For days thereafter the Arabs talked of nothing else. Naturally, the story spread and the surrounding country was beginning to be intensely interested in what is quite common in Africa – nerve thrilling accounts of the resurrection of the dead. We never exposed the young humorist, for we knew that a sudden and swift revenge would be his lot at the hands of outraged natives.

The Arab takes unnatural phenomena quite seriously. He has no particular desire to see a ghost, or to hear one, but having once been so privileged, his wrath would be fearful indeed should he discover that the ghosts were man-made. After all, he is the representative of an old race and would find slight pleasure in being spoofed by an enthusiastic American youth.

From Touggourt we sped southwest to Ouargla (Wargla),[1] where we were greeted by the French officers of the picturesque garrison – "the real Saharans" – who have adapted their lives to the demands of the desert, with its hardships and solitude. We had our last big party at the "popote," the officers' dining hall, and spent the last hours in civilization in talking of our hopes of discoveries, of the food caravans that had gone on ahead, and of all the general precautions to be taken to insure the safety of the endeavor.

At dawn we collected in front of the statue of the ill-fated Colonel Flatters and in the presence of the commander of the garrison, the officers, and several hundred natives, we

---

1.   It must be borne in mind that African towns not infrequently bear two or three different spellings. In this book the author has followed, where possible, the better known form.

attached our French and American pennants to the giant cars and rolled away for deepest Sahara.

For many weary miles the trail followed the dried-out water course of the Oed Mia. In the past the water had cut out a great depression, leaving vast terraces of multi-colored chalk and stone, as vivid in color as the canyons of the Colorado. On the banks of this dead river we collected many beautiful flints of the prehistoric neolithic age – spearheads, arrowheads, stone hatchets and many marvelous flints of a forgotten age, when the great river flowed here and when plant life and dense jungle covered the now desolate desert.

Not far from Ouargla one perceives the famous landmark, the Gara Krima,[1] at whose sight the Saharans all rejoice, for it marks "the arrival" after crossing the long tracks of desolation. How many are the weary eyes that have gazed with insuperable joy at that table mountain which can be seen for a radius of thirty miles.

With a small party, we climbed the rocky fastness, on whose summit are the ruins of an ancient Berber fortress of the Tenth Century, though the foundations probably are far more ancient. The summit of the Gara Krima is accessible only by a narrow rock path that passes through the ruins of an ancient doorway. Neolithic flints are still to be found on the plateau above, showing that it served as a defense citadel in prehistoric times.

On the plateau we located the famous well that has been the problem of many archaeologists. The well is two hundred feet deep, cut through the solid rock of the mountain to some distance below the desert level. It is difficult to imagine how this laborious undertaking was accomplished and we can never know how long it took the laborers, working, as they did, with crude flint tools. But it must have been a work of years. The undertaking, of course, was necessitous,

---

1.　Called by desert people "The Rainbow of the Sahara," a name supplied by the vivid multi-colored formation of its perpindicular sides.

for it insured the dwellers of the citadel a limitless supply of water in time of siege.

While exploring the regions in the neighborhood of this old deserted fortress, we found a perfect Chellean *"coup de poing,"* (flint hatchet) two hundred thousand to three hundred thousand years old! It was a perfect specimen and proved to us that, since the dawn of time, man had lived there.

Near the place where we found this stone hatchet we made a discovery that is still a mystery – a large field of cinders and ashes under a layer of sand. It looked as if a great fort had once burned down, for we followed the traces of these black ashes for several miles. That night we camped under the stars, not far from the well of Hassi Berkan and had our first introduction to the bitter cold of the Saharan nights. The day had been very hot, and our thermometer registered 70 degrees difference between midday and midnight.

At dawn we arose, somewhat stiffly, I recall, and followed the dried-out river bed of the Oed Moussa. On one of the terraces we found a prehistoric site which yielded us several hundred flints. These we photographed, filmed, and packed away in the specially made specimen boxes.

Several times on the long trail from Ouargla to Hassi Inifel we noticed the graves of those who had died of thirst or in the many battles between Tuareg and Chaamba. To our left we began to see the sand dunes of the Erg Oriental, which form a billowing sea of sand for hundreds of miles to the east. What a stupendous spectacle they make, especially at dawn when the rising sun tips their silvery summits with fingers of fire and the purple night shadows at their bases fade into the lighter colors of the clear early morning azure of a Saharan day.

In the vicinity of Hassi Inifel the dunes rise to great heights like some Alpine panorama, vast, seemingly endless, and so majestic that one feels dwarf-like and infinitesimal. The sublime spectacle remains imprinted in the mind forever. We were so enchanted at the fairy scene that greeted us at Hassi Inifel, coming, as it did, after the long and weary three hundred and fifty kilometers from Ouargla, that we stopped the cars above the precipices of the dead river and gazed in rapturous awe at this inspiring sight.

The abandoned fortress of Hassi Inifel is surrounded by encroaching sands, which in time will swallow the outpost and well, unless some precautions are taken to protect this site. We used one of the mighty rooms of the *bordj* as a headquarters while exploring this region. Our gasoline and food supplies were awaiting us, guarded by two military Goumier Meharists, mounted on their beautiful white giant Mehari camels. We found, to our dismay and chagrin, that forty per cent of our gasoline had evaporated in its six hundred kilometer camel ride from Touggourt. Due to the intense heat, added to the motion of the camels, the tins and cylinders had leaked badly. One of the great problems of desert motor travel, both in Asia and Africa, is the question of how to prevent the evaporation of gasoline when it is being transported hundreds of miles in advance of the expedition. The recent Roy Chapman Andrews expedition to the Gobi Desert suffered from this problem.

While camping at Hassi Inifel, a small party explored the sand dune region to the east and had the satisfaction of finding a rich prehistoric site in the heart of a sand mountain. It was here that we climbed a dune fourteen hundred and sixty feet in height, one of the highest, I think, ever ascended in the Sahara, though some of those seen in the Libyan desert appeared as high, if not higher. We took a film of the crossing of this dune. With our Alpenstocks (I carry one as an arm as well as a tool for probing and climbing) we looked much as if we were setting out on an expedition to the snow-capped ledges of Mount Blanc.

Recently there has been quite a controversy regarding these sand dunes. Mr. Gautier, Mr. Ball, and Mr. Beadnell all hold different theories as to their origin and history. Professor Gautier is of the opinion that the dunes of the Sahara are more or less stationary, but this does not seem quite in keeping with known facts, especially when one considers how quickly the sand advances on abandoned oases, deserted cities, and buildings put up only a few years ago. Indeed, the encroaching sands around the fortress of Hassi Inifel seem to disprove Gautier's theory.

While exploring the prehistoric site east of our camp, we were surprised to note that the great dunes covered large areas where, in neolithic times, a large population must have existed. The human artifacts lie on the rock surface of the desert and in the plain. We had to dig into the dunes, where a special deposit was located. In the region southwest of Siwa we remarked the same strange fact; the ancient civilization was being slowly covered by the advancing sand from the east. Among the dunes of the Erg Oriental, some of the mountains of sand had completely crossed a site of ancient habitation and here the hand-wrought flints were again uncovered. It is difficult to calculate how many thousands of years this process must have taken, but it is at least certain that it has been indeed long, for the millions of tons of sand move only under the propulsion of the terrific desert winds.

In the eager search for traces of early man in the Erg west of Hassi Inifel, Henri Barth and I became separated from the rest of the party. Due to the sudden failing of light that comes at evening, we found ourselves in the dark among endless sand dunes of puzzling infinity. To add to our discomfort a bitter wind chilled us to the marrow. The realization that a cold night in the dunes was to be our lot was not a particularly cheering prospect.

After several hours of traveling up and down the mountains of sand in the direction in which we knew the camp lay, we at last saw the flashlights of the cars criss-crossing the night sky. It was indeed a welcome beacon to guide us home. We arrived late at night, fairly exhausted, for the climbing had been hard and we had burdened ourselves with many heavy flints.

Next morning we visited the cemetery of Hassi Inifel, where lie the bones of the murdered "White Fathers" of Cardinal Lavigerie.[1] The great Primate of Africa had sent several of his heroic missionaries into the Sahara to carry the word of God to the savages, but their death was another tragic chapter in the history of the Christian efforts to civilize the Tuareg. The three brave souls who lie in the little stone enclosure were butchered in their tents. They carried no arms and no money, and they died merely because they were Christians and aliens. The "Forgotten of God," though bearing on their shields and trappings the sign of the Cross,[2] know it only as an ornament, and their blood lust does not spare the lives of those followers of the Cross who, actuated by high purpose, come here with a two century old story to tell these truly abandoned of God.

We also visited the Koubba (tomb of the desert sands) where the famous battle took place between the Tuareg and their hereditary enemies, the Chaamba. The Tuareg assassins captured here were taken to Algiers, where they were kept as "specimens for study" by the professors of Algiers, for up to that time even the Tuareg cranial measurements were unknown.[3]

Soon after leaving Hassi Inifel on our three hundred and fifty kilometer advance south to Ain Guettara, we passed a spot in the dunes where we saw the remains of an airplane that had fallen in a sand storm, while out on a patrol to locate a marauding band of Tuareg raiders. The plane had crashed some time during the late world war.

We camped that night, October 20, at Merjouma, after descending through wild gorges to the dried-out water bed of the upper reaches of the Oed Mia. The following morning

---

1. 1875. Fathers Paulmier, Menoret and Bouchard, all decapitated.

2. See Chapter "The People of the Veil," for further comment.

3. P. Vuillot. *Exploration du Sahara*, Paris, 1895.

I made an early reconnaissance of this region. While climbing a mountain overlooking the dead river I had the good fortune to discover the remarkable collection of ancient Libyan inscriptions, which we afterwards named the "Love Mountain." The mountain was literally covered with Tifinar inscriptions of great antiquity. By the aid of Belaid, our Tuareg interpreter, we were able to decipher a number of them. Others were of such great age that we could do no more than copy them for future study by the Abbé Chabot, a member of the French Institute and foremost Liby-Phoenician scholar. We had a delightful time reading these old love messages of a forgotten people, who must have selected this particular mountain as a trysting place. Such child-like messages as "Lili loves Bellzar," "Matouki is still waiting for Rzzohra" (let us hope that the long wait is now ended), "Eternal love for Dashi," and one especially pathetic message, "I have surely said to you all that I can."

For hours we drew, photographed and filmed this romantic mountain, lost in the distant reaches of the now desolate, abandoned, sun-scorched, devil region of the "Tadmait." Could such passionate love, we wondered, ever have burned in this arid region? Did the lovers of the dim day know the shadowed retreat of fronded palm gardens? Is it possible that their messages of love engraved in imperishable stone is more lasting than the very face of nature itself?

One of the amazing things which we noted were the hundreds of footprints carved into the rock on the edge of the precipices and terraces of this Love Mountain. A Tuareg noble, Babe Ag Tamaklas, told me (and I have heard it elsewhere) that these outlines of feet drawings were love, or marriage pacts. He explained that the marriage vow was perpetuated by drawings being taken of the feet of the bride and bridegroom, and their names inscribed around the drawing with the vow of eternal fidelity written in between. There were no thumb prints taken in those days, and I doubt if the footprints were enough to bind the sailor-like travelers of the Sahara, centuries ago.

Our interpreter told us another legend dealing with these mysterious rock carvings. He said that the Tuareg brave used to chase his well-beloved to some precipice and there, while she was making a great show of being about to plunge herself to death upon the rocks below, would promise eternal fidelity and everlasting love. It must be borne in mind that the Tuareg woman is the suitor, and it is quite natural that the love-sick Tuareg brave, finding his beloved about to dash herself to death, would swear to anything. It is a dire situation for any man to be placed in even in this day. In many cases their footprints would then and there be carved in the rock probably by some enterprising Tuareg parson living on the mountain and holding himself ready for just such an emergency and the lovers were bound forever. Let us pay the tribute of believing that they lived happy ever after.

Some of the inscriptions which we found on the mountain were superimposed on other more ancient drawings, showing that the mountain was used through the ages for these love pacts. Even the scientist, who by many is supposed to be more or less insensible to human emotions, will find himself drawing upon his imagination and upon the past. He will picture in his own mind some beautiful Tuareg maiden, poised on the precipice of the mountain, with the desert wind blowing her black tresses, while the warrior at her feet is swearing his devotion on the hilt of his two-handed sword, even as did the knights of medieval days.

While following the course of the Oed Mia, we explored a number of caves on the towering heights above the ancient water-bed and were overjoyed to discover a series of beautiful rock drawings made by prehistoric artists. Pictures of antelopes, giraffes, a buffalo, and several other indistinct animals and figures were copied from the walls at the back of the caves.

From Merjouma we blazed a trail across the weird, sun-blackened region of the Tadmait plateau, perhaps one of the most dreary regions on earth. It is here that one hears that strange phenomenon of the Sahara – the rifle-like bursting of the rocks. Due to the great heat of the day and the sudden dropping of temperature to freezing point at night, the swift change causes the stones to burst. The Tuareg say it is the evil spirits, the Djinns, warning that war is ahead and that one must not sleep, for enemies are on the trail with intent to kill.

In crossing the Tadmait we met the military patrol that was returning north after accompanying our supply train south. They told us of a rumor in the Sahara of a raid being prepared to overtake the expedition when it reached the "Land of Fear," the desolate Tanezrouft region. Later we learned that such indeed was the case, but that the raiders from Morocco had missed us by only a few miles, while we were southwest of the Hoggar.

At Ain Guettara we descended the gorges where one of the most dreadful massacres of the late war took place and where a small fortress had been built immediately after the disaster to prevent the possibility of such an ambush again. Adjutant Chapuis, one of my guides, had been first on the scene after the massacre and explained the whole dreadful tragedy to us on the actual spot. The story is this:

Several motor cars were winding their way down to the canyon below, where the fresh water well is located, when suddenly the foremost car was held up by a barrier of stone. It was immediately greeted by a fusillade of shots. The attack was sudden and surprising. Panic overtook the soldiers. They sought escape in all directions from the pitiless fire of the hidden Tuareg. Several actually plunged over the edge of the precipice and were instantly killed on the rocks below. The officer in command made one of those heroic struggles that make epic history of desert warfare. He managed to reach the plateau above and, finding cover behind a few stones, made a glorious stand against the Tuareg.

When Chapuis found his body, two days later, it was riddled with bullets. Several hundred empty cartridge shells lay about in the sand. He had sold his life dearly, for Chapuis found the hastily made graves of several Tuareg and Senussi in one of the lonely canyons where the raiders had buried their dead before disappearing into the desert. Traces of the tragedy were still to be seen; the twisted steel of the burned cars, pieces of wood and other relics still lie in the dark, gloomy canyon where the attack was made ten years ago.

There is a beautiful well at Ain Guettara, below the monument that covers the dead soldiers of France. It is a clear running source of water. This is a rare thing in the Sahara, and it provided us with a bath after long days without such comfort. We drew lots as to the succession in which we would take our plunge and I had the ill fortune to draw the twelfth and last lot.

While the motor cars were being overhauled, oiled and examined, we explored several caves in the picturesque valley, one of which was an *"abri sous roche,"* with implements resembling the Tardenoisien civilization. There is no doubt that this oasis was once a great center of human habitation, due to its beautiful well, surrounded by tall palm trees, and the numerous natural rock shelters. There was still an old guardian at the abandoned fortress who complained bitterly that trade was very bad and that, barring the Citroen expedition two years previous, no one had come that way to relieve his loneliness. We left him some tea and sugar, and advised him to go up North where he might expect at least one or two expeditions a year to trade with. His was the least exertive or exciting life imaginable, a real example of how little a human being can do in this world and still exist.

South of Ain Guettara we passed the tombs of an entire family who had died of thirst the year before. First the mother had collapsed, then the children, and last of all the father, who struggled to within half a mile of the well before his poor soul gave up. Such is the trail of the desert, an endless tale of sorrow, of bloodshed and thirst, of sufferings and struggles, unequalled perhaps in any other region of the globe for dramatic intensity.

The trail from Ain Guettara to In Salah is long and wearisome. Dreary miles of sun-blasted rocks, scorching canyons and sandy plains simmering in the torrid air greeted us on every side. A half day's journey south of Ain Guettara we came to a dried-out lake. We explored what had once been an island and found there numerous paleolithic *"coup de poing."* There must have been giants in those days, for some of the work instruments were very large and of great weight.

We tried to visualize the combats between man and beast in those dawn-days. The great Cayman then existed all over the Sahara and even to-day crocodiles still exist in some of the swamp lands of the Hoggar. Several have been found recently, but with the cobra and elephant they belong to the fauna of the Southlands, remnants of an age when Saharan rivers watered the land, and when the desolate wastes we were now crossing were dense jungles.

On the way to In Salah we passed a giant meteorite which is held in great veneration and superstition by the Tuareg. Meteorites are called "star messengers" by the Tuareg.

We arrived in the Tidikelt late at night and in the darkness missed the fortress of In Salah. For hours we circled round and round until at last we saw a great flashlight leap out of the night to lead us to the fort. From a high tower the officers of the desert outpost had seen the flashlights of the cars circling around in the desert like lost fireflies. The officers came out to meet us and we had a great reception, for to them a visit was indeed an event. Champagne and wines were immediately brought forth and we made merry until the small hours, even indulging in an impromptu dance to the sound of "It ain't goin' to rain no more, no more" played on our small portable phonograph.

Lieutenant Triollet, Doctor Nicolle and several others made our visit to the desert fortress as enjoyable as possible. We had brought the longed-for mail from France six weeks ahead of the time they were expecting it, and to those poor beings, cut off from the outside world, this was their great joy.

Lieutenant Fenieux, whom we had brought from Tougourt as an exchange officer, had the cafard before he even reached the headquarters where he was to serve for the next two years in this lonely "Kingdom of the Sand". The cafard is the dreadful sickness of ennui, in other words homesickness of a most virulent nature brought on by the terrible loneliness of Saharan outpost life. To have the cafard after several months in the desert is both reasonable and expected, but to get it before arriving at your post is quite unpardonable. An acute attack of this illness is sometimes mortal. Young men, accustomed to city life and home, have committed suicide rather than endure the ghastly, utter loneliness of the interminable desert spaces.

You either love the Sahara and pardon its roughness, or you hate it, as did poor Lieutenant Fenieux from the first moment he laid his eyes upon it. The officers at In Salah told us humorous and pathetic tales of how the members of the command get on one another's nerves. Sometimes they do not speak to each other for weeks, following some utterly trivial incident, and everything seems to irritate them. Those who have seen the play, "White Cargo," know what desert cafard is like. In the tropics it is "damp rot" that gets into one's soul; in the Sahara it is the silence and monotony that brings on a boredom that is fatal to some.

At In Salah, Lieutenant Triollet informed us that a wireless had come from the north to inform him that a great "rezzou" had left from the mountains of Morocco and was on the way across the Sahara. The raiders, it seemed, were several hundred strong and for many days we were in fear that orders would come forbidding the expedition to proceed. However, no further news of the raiders arrived and we left In Salah with strict instructions to maintain a sharp outlook for the marauders and to keep our machine gun continually mounted and prepared.

We now crossed the vast plains of the Tidikelt, once part of the Tuareg domain but now rarely visited by the veiled people. In the region of Hassi-el-Khenig we passed the remains of petrified forests half buried in the sand. They made me think of the petrified forest in the Libyan Desert that an explorer mistook a hundred years ago for the masts of dead ships!

In the region between the desert fortress of In Salah and the great plateau of the Mouydir I saw several fossil deposits that we marked with cairns for removal on our return journey.

The land was beginning to rise now. We were approaching the roof of the Sahara – the great mountain ranges of the mysterious Hoggar. Desert shrubs and plants were becoming more numerous in the beds of the dead rivers and we daily hunted the gazelle for fresh food. Many times the gazelles would stop directly in front of us. So surprised were they to see us, and to hear a motor car for the first time, that their curiosity overcame their fear. The poor beasts are shot down easily in such case, a thing we did only when in need of food. They are such graceful, beautiful beasts that there is no sport in killing them. In fact, one wonders why the word "sport" is applied to the useless slaughter of game.

Yet there are expeditions that go out by the dozens to slaughter by hundreds the beautiful wild game of Africa. Every time I see some big game hunter's picture in the paper, surrounded by his trophies proof of his marksmanship – I get a severe "pain in the neck." It seems a poor thing to be proud of, this hunting with a dozen powerful guns and scores of natives. Massacre is massacre, wherever it takes place, and it is particularly objectionable when we consider that the wonderful and beautiful wild animal life is being wiped out in the name of "sport."

There are few things so pleasing to the eye as a flock of gazelles, running and jumping gracefully across the desert plains. They seem actually to want to play with you. They jump around, nibble playfully at the bushes, kick out their heels in mock combat, wag their heads and give you a parting salute with a flip of their white tails. Those tails, alas! give them away; they are snow white and can be seen from afar in the desert brush. A herd of gazelles provides a spectacle never to be forgotten when outlined on the top of a ridge against the blue sky or seen sometimes by the score, flying across the desert at an incredible speed, like a cloud of swallows flying low.

On the trails through the deserts of the Tidikelt one is astonished at the number of dead and mummified camels passed on the way. The caravan route is lined with these faithful servitors of the desert people. They serve their masters from an early age, only to die abandoned. And oh, wretched thought! they generally die from thirst and exhaustion. Theirs is a sad lot. They seem born to suffer eternally and perhaps that is why they have such a sad look and are always complaining when a load is put on their backs. I can well understand the grief of the Scotch explorer, Mr. Buchanan, when his faithful camel died at Touggourt after carrying him across the Sahara in 1924.[1]

Some people laugh at the thought that you can have an affection for a camel, but I shall never forget some of my desert animal friends. The camel is fully as intelligent as the horse, and has what we call "camel sense." He is peculiarly fitted for his desert life, and you must study him closely to find all his special traits. A camel has certain unerring instincts and will locate water in an uncanny way. Many a

---

1. *Sahara*, by Angus Buchanan, London, 1926.

tragedy has been caused by camels being left untied at night and leaving their masters to return to some distant well. They are known to have abandoned a caravan that is going through a waterless desert and to return to some distant well many miles away. They are vindictive beasts at times and always remember an injury, even to the point of attempting to trample on a man who has maltreated them.

A mad camel is a sight not easy to forget and to see a battle between two giant males, in the mating season, is a spectacle that would satisfy even an ancient Roman audience. We once filmed such a fight, which ended with the final piercing of the jugular vein after a long struggle of entwined necks and slowly advancing pitiless teeth.

Near the Oed Khenig we saw the pathetic spectacle of a camel lying dead with his teeth buried in the base of a palm tree that had been placed in the desert as a landmark. The poor beast, dying of thirst, had instinctively tried to get some moisture from what he knew had once been a tree. There are thousands and thousands of white, bleaching bones in this region – the remains of beasts of burden who could not quite survive the long crossing of the Sahara, to reach the longed-for wells of In Salah.

The first view of the Mouydir region is impressive; out of the plains rise the first mountains of the Central Plateau like a mirage of strange purple masses of rocks. The mighty, legendary Mount Oudane is the first sentinel-like volcano of the towering Hoggar range to be seen on the distant horizon. The desert air is so clear that the range seems close at hand, but the journey was long before we reached the red and black cliffs and camped near the beautiful well of Tesnou, under the frowning heights. The well is located in an ancient river bed. We reached it in the dark, disturbing numerous wild animals who make it their desert watering place. A mountain goat was outlined against the amphitheatre of rocks that surrounds the well, but in a flash he was gone. Next morning we arose early and swam in the cool depths, after having first filled the water tanks and "girbas" with the life-giving fluid, in preparation for the long miles still ahead of us.

In following a river bed in the direction of Amjid, the well where the last of the Flatters' expedition died, we saw many rock drawings of great antiquity, and a number of modern ones showing we were now in the domain of the Tuareg. On the summits of the Mountains of Tefedest we noticed that small cairns of stones had been built, sites marking the battlefield of the Chaamba and Tuareg, we were told, but they were also used as a secret signal system of the Tuareg.

For two days we passed along the base of the Great Plateau of the Mouydir, a wall of rock rising a thousand feet above the plain. The Tuareg have many legends and superstitions in regard to these unscaled plateaux and of the legendary Mount Oudane. They say that the evil spirits of the Sahara live up in those unexplored heights, great hordes of Djinns who come down in the form of sand storms and whirlwinds and are the spirits that sing among the dunes.

According to the Tuareg, Mount Oudane is the famous mountain of the beautiful women spirits, a sort of Amazon people who have a mysterious city upon the heights, with date and palm trees and beautiful palaces. Like the sirens of old, they are supposed to entice the noble young Tuaregs up into the mountain and, of course, they are never seen again. It is the home of Antinea, the legendary descendant of Neptune's daughter, last of the lost Atlantis people who, in Pierre Benoit's novel, used to entice explorers to her domain where they died of love and were then turned into stone to adorn a marble hall filled with numerous sweethearts. There are several sacred mountains in Africa, such as Bou Kornein, the twin-horned, temple-crowned mountain that looks across the Gulf of Tunis to the ruins of ancient Carthage. On its summit was a temple of Baal – the same kind of "high place" that is often mentioned in the Bible, and which originated in the distant land of Canaan. The Greeks, too, say that Hercules held up the Atlas Mountains, and at El Kantara you can still see the mountains cleft in twain by the mighty sword of Hercules. Mount Adrian, in the heart of the Hoggar, which I climbed, was also cut in twain by the mythical Tuareg giant, Eleas.

The explorer, Richardson, was lost while exploring the Ksar Djennoun near Rhat, and Barth nearly died of thirst climbing among the rock pinnacles of this castle of "the desert spirits." In the far-off Libyan Desert, is the Djebel Sekunder, Alexander the Great's mountain, where the Macedonian conqueror lost his way on his journey to the Oasis of Jupiter-Ammon. Mount Illiman, according to the Tuareg, holds up the sky of the Hoggar, and Gara Krima, because of its vivid rock colorations, is called the "fiancé of the rainbow." It is strange to think that the mythical legends of the Greeks, and the Phoenicians, still have their origin in the modern legend of the desert people to-day.

While camping under the lee of Mount Tesnou we saw on many of the rocks in the region fine examples of primitive drawings, including those of elephants, which were perfect in dimension and style. There are no elephants within a thousand miles of this spot now, and we wondered when they were last seen in the Sahara. Naturally, Hannibal, Hasdrubal and Hamilcar, and other Carthaginian generals, must have destroyed many thousands of African elephants in their great campaigns. We know that the Romans hunted them mercilessly in the Oed Rhir so as to supply the vast amphitheatres of Africa and Rome with the popular and gigantic beast.

The demand in Africa must have been very great for such spectacles, and the astonishing amphitheatre of El Djem, the ancient Thysdrus in Tunisia, is a standing proof of how animal battles and the baiting of Christians were conducted on a large scale. That amphitheatre, now in ruinous perfection, was as large as the Colosseum at Rome, held

eighty thousand spectators and is standing to-day in the
desert region of North Africa.

Perhaps, too, the elephants we saw engraved on the
rocks of Tesnou were memories of the day when these beasts
of burden were used on the ancient Saharan caravan trails
before the advent of the camel.[1] There was more water in
those days, and slaves, gold, ivory and emeralds were sought
for by the rich Carthaginians and Romans in this land of the
ancient Garamantians and Ethiopians. It is probable that
there were caravans of elephants in those days, in place of
the picturesque camel trains of to-day.

When we reached Tesnou we found that seventy per cent
of our gasoline had evaporated and, worse still, the well that
we were counting on had dried up, due to the sand having
been trampled into it by camels, and perhaps by men. In the
old days, the Tuareg often kept their kingdom inviolate by
destroying the wells before approaching strangers.

That night of disappointment we camped at the entrance
of the gorge of Arak, the valley of the evil spirits, a majestic
canyon with towering precipices of weather-toned pinnacles
of rock. The Tuareg and Arab will not sleep in that deep and
mysterious canyon, for they claim that every night the
dreaded Djinns throw great boulders down on the sleeping
or passing caravan. Due to the great difference between tem-
peratures at night and day the rocks break away and come
roaring down into the valley. All night long we heard small
avalanches crashing down from the crags, awakening endless weird echoes in this gloomy canyon.

At dawn we collected our energies so as to try to make
the pass in a day, but after one of those typical days of desert
hardship we were still caught in the gorges at night. We had
to make trail in many places, to get the heavy cars across
deep depressions caused by previous torrential rains. For
hours we worked in the blazing heat of the fiery, rock

---

1.   Frobernius, *Hadsha Maktuba.*

enclosed valley, removing the hot rocks or filling endless holes with them. The moving pictures give a graphic view of our work in this region.

At midday we reached an enormous boulder in the heart of the canyon where we expected to find water, but alas! the well was again dried up and the party was now absolutely waterless! The evil spirits of the Hoggar were beginning to play their tricks and when we reached the fourth well and found that non-existent I began to feel really anxious for the welfare of the expedition I was leading into the Hoggar.

What with our disappointment in finding no water and the continual efforts to get the tire-punctured cars through the gorges in the blazing heat, our tempers were on edge. As is well known, noise of any sort will often start an avalanche in the Alps where the rocks are balanced, so to speak, half in the air, and it has often been a wonder to me how the lusty language in French, English, Tuareg and Arab, used while getting our cars through the canyon of Arak, did not start a series of landslides on top of us.

It was up one of the lesser canyons of these great gorges, at a well called Inzize, that Chapuis reported having found a well with fish in it; Saharan fish in the heart of the desert![1] But we found no water, and, therefore, no fish. Several members of the party were beginning to suffer seriously from thirst. Henri Barth, our movie operator, being of large girth and not quite up to roughing it to such an extent, complained that if he had known he was to emulate the camel he would have taken on more water at the last well.

After camping under the cliffs of Arak we made an early start so that we might reach a well which our guide Chapuis knew of in the heart of a distant mountain range. On the way we stopped in a valley called Tiritimin, where our motor cars crossed a long stretch of smooth rock, marked with thousands of Libyan inscriptions, a truly unexpected and aston-

---

1.   See Duveyrier, *Le Tuareg du Nord.*

ishing spectacle. Despite our suffering, we spent several hours photographing and filming this sacred spot of the ancient desert people.

By now all our muscles were aching and our faces were blistered with sun and windburn. We were very thirsty and several of us were suffering from badly poisoned feet, caused by the long sharp needles of a sort of desert plant that grew profusely in this canyon. Every few hundred yards our motor tires would be pierced by these needle-like spikes and we were continually pumping up tires. My own feet soon became swollen to twice their normal size and I knew that the others suffered. The natural grandeur of the scene, however, helped us forget our petty miseries and we felt it a privilege to pass through a magic land of such natural beauty as was to be seen on every hand in this surprising valley of the evil spirits.

At last we reached a canyon where another well was supposed to be located, but it lay far up a rocky valley that was as hot as the door to Hades. We left the motors behind and carried with us all our water tanks and bottles in case of good luck. Two or three of us reached the well first and immediately buried our faces in the cool water. It was a never-to-be-forgotten moment of exquisite, unalloyed bliss. To our dying day we shall never forget that drink, and I thought we would never stop lapping up the precious liquid. It is really worth while going several days in the desert without water, to enjoy the ecstasy that comes when thirst can at last be assuaged.

We had to carry the water from this blessed mountain well a distance of two miles, which took many long hours of tramping in the blazing sun. We filled up the radiators, all the tanks, all our bottles and skins, and then drank as much as we could. It had been a good lesson to us and taught me never again to rely on supposed wells, even to those marked on the official military maps!

Before reaching the first Tuareg village of In Amejel, Chapuis located another well, one of the most romantically located Saharan sources I ever have seen. We were passing a great solid wall of rock mountain when suddenly this old sand-dog skipper of the desert pointed at a certain spot and exclaimed that there was water over there. We drove the car to the spot indicated and to our surprise found a fissure in the rock into which Chapuis and Belaid promptly and mysteriously disappeared. After hunting around a while we found the entrance and almost on hands and knees followed a long, cool passage in the tracks of the two vanished Saharans.

Our electric torches became useful until suddenly a shaft of light, coming from a fissure far overhead, lit up a beautiful pool of emerald water in the heart of the mountain! Strange inscriptions covered the walls and we saw the prints of Tuareg sandals mixed with those of the jackal, gazelle and birds imprinted in the snow-white sand around the pool. The place was so strange that we spoke in whispers, which echoed and re-echoed in the dim passages of this ancient mountain known since the dawn of time by the desert folk, both human and animal.

We sat there silently smoking our pipes and wondering over all the surprises that this mysterious man Chapuis was forever revealing to us. How cool it was as we came in from the blasting heat of the desert floor! We stretched our tired muscles and car-cramped limbs in the soft powder-like sand and from time to time lazily bent over to drink the cool water with the extravagant and blissful feeling that we could drink all we wanted. We began to dream about the secret pool and our imaginations went into the realms of fancy to the days when the pirates of the desert must have used this retreat as a hidden resting place.

We saw the rich caravans of old, bearing the gold dust and emeralds of the mines of the Garamantians to adorn the lovely ladies of ancient Carthage and Rome. Further back we could picture the prehistoric hunters using the cave and preparing their flint knives and adzes by the opalescent waters of the life-giving pool. A few ostrich shells, bits of old cloth and matting, a few whitened bones, and innumerable writings on the walls were all that remained on the surface, but we longed to dig out the sand-filled passage on the further side of the pool in the hope that it might reveal a hidden treasure of a forgotten people. But time was precious and we must regretfully leave this lonely desert haunt and face the heat and wind of the outside world if we were to reach Atakor, the high central plateau of the Hoggar.

I shall never forget the sudden view of the needle-like towering mountains of the land of the Tuareg that greeted our astonished eyes on emerging from the enclosed canyons that had hidden our view. Imagine a group of purple and mauve mountains forming a collection of pinnacled heights reaching far up into the bluest of skies, with their bases seeming to float in the mists of the simmering, sun-dancing sand vapors. If ever there existed a lost Atlantis, it must have looked something like this, a great island of precipitous rocks where, amongst cascades and flowers and marble temples, lived a legendary people of whom all antiquity once spoke in glowing terms.

It was a thrilling moment and we gazed in awe on the mysterious land of our hopes and dreams. Our impatience was great as we felt that the goal was near, and we put on full speed to reach before nightfall the enveloping shadows of the legendary mountain. The great mountains of Tahat and Illiman, the kings of the Atakor, rise eleven thousand feet above the desert and majestically dominate the group. As we approached the scene shifted rapidly, like a succession of ever changing tableaux. More and more peaks appeared, like vast giants rising up suddenly out of the desert, and as night fell upon us we felt as if it were all a dream and that no such place could really exist.

As the sun reached the horizon the peaks became lit with the vivid Saharan twilight flames that change from moment to moment into kaleidoscopic rainbow colors. Night falls swiftly in the Sahara and the vivid tones softened into delicate crimsons and purple shadows tinged with lilac. Suddenly, imperceptibly, the glorious panorama faded into the velvety darkness and the desert night fell on us, a silent group, who felt that for one brief moment we had stood on the threshold of another world.

That night we camped under the star-emblazoned Hoggar heaven. In the clear, clean mountain air the twinkling lights of the firmament seem so close that you feel you could reach up and touch them. It was late before we slept that night, for the Tuareg serfs had given us a noisy welcome at the stockaded village of In Amejel. They danced around us with drums beating, accompanied by many a wild, barbaric chant, reminiscent of the shrill cries of the ancient Libyans described by Herodotus.

We saw for the first time the Tuareg sword dance which we later filmed at the dead of night with special flares that lit up the haunting scene – a strange picture that will remain forever in our memories. We fell asleep at last, hearing in the distance the muffled dull beating of a Tuareg drum and feeling that we were on the threshold of a savage, unknown world. . .

And so we were. After all the hardship, and all the beauty, we were at last among "The People of the Veil" a noble, yet savage, brave, yet heartless race, whose origin no man knoweth and who walk proudly in their fierce and fearless majesty.

Chapter 4

"THE PEOPLE OF THE VEIL"

"Ten days' journey beyond the Garamantiens there is another highland with salt and water, and there live the people called Atarantes. They curse the sun, whose heat is excessive, and have many maledictions against it for making their land and themselves miserable.

"Ten days beyond is another highland of salt and water where men live. Near this mass of salt, is the mountain that is called Atlas. It is from this mountain that the inhabitants of this land derive their name, for they are called Atlantes. . ."

— Herodotus (550 B.C.)

Few regions of the world are as strange and wild as the home of the Tuareg in the heart of the Saharan Alps – the brooding, mysterious Hoggar. This volcanic region resembles nothing so much as a lunar panorama. Imagine a land of towering mountains whose peaks are needle-pointed, glistening black in the clear mountain air and closely resembling thousands of gigantic minarets or vast mediaeval towers and battlements. And they frown down upon all those who are alien to the land. Far back in the fastness of their impregnable heights are dark and gloomy canyons set with a few trees and desert plants and it is there that you find the tents of the truly "Abandoned of God"!

The silence is appalling; in the crystalline mountain air sounds are magnified as nowhere else on earth. As you approach a Tuareg camp you are generally met, not greeted, by one of the tall, majestic nobles. They are suspicious of strangers, (they have a right to be) and like the American Indian they wait for you to speak first.

We ask if we may visit the encampment – a thing I detest doing – but we must swallow our inhibitions for we are here to study a little-known people. Quite naturally, they resent being regarded as so many animals in a zoo, for it must be borne in mind that they are the knights and nobles of the desert.

I have often wondered how I would feel toward strangers who came suddenly and unannounced into my own home to begin an investigation into the mode and manner of my living. I might refrain from booting them out, but I am quite sure my resentment would rise considerably should any such stranger be graceless enough to display a humorous interest in my customs!

However, the Tuareg was quite hospitable and we sat down to a cup of tea! But the social amenities ended there and we became the focus of the great black, kohl-painted eyes of the veiled giants who, wordless, gazed steadfastly at us. Now, suddenly, the tables were turned and we were the objects of interest.

There is no question but what one feels the malignity that envelops the hidden personality of the Tuareg, and at such times it is surprisingly easy to recall the deathdealing spear that traversed Reygasse's tent one silent night, or the tombs of Palat and Douls and Flatters, far out in the sands, or, what is far more tragic because of its nearness to me, the passing of some of my own brave comrades, killed by Tuareg as I write these lines.[1]

---

1.   Capts. Debenne, Pasquet, Resset, and Gen. Clavery. They were massacred on the road to Beni Abbes, December, 1928. As I read these proofs, news comes of another disaster at Ain Yacoub, (S. Morocco) wherein 83 French officers and men are killed.

Duveyrier may call them "Knights of the Desert," Mr. F. R. Rodd may speak of them as "his good friends," but behind the veil masking their faces is the hate of ages and I confess that I felt it ever when in their presence. Whatever their outward actions, however gracious their manner (and they can be as courtly as any "parfit, gentil knight") nevertheless I could not put from my mind the historical fact that the Sahara is spotted by marked and unmarked graves – mute testimony that the Tuareg holds the desert to be his own and strikes hard and swift when he feels that trespassers are violating his rights.

The Tuareg life is nomadic, for they have a superstition that it will bring misfortune if they sleep under a real roof. The noble Tuareg is not an agriculturist. He disdains the toil of the soil – "it is the work of negroes and slaves," he says, and their camps, therefore, are always on the trail.[1] Their tents are never grouped close together but are situated several hundred yards apart, generally in the lee of some wind-protected boulder.

I shall never forget the Tuareg camp that we found in the wild "Valley of the Giants." The great rocks in this valley had been moulded into fantastic forms by the winds of ages. The continual wearing of their bases by the sand-laden winds had made monuments of stone, lightly balanced at the bases, and many of them took on the grotesque forms of prehistoric monsters. In the moonlight they are really quite terrifying.

This "Valley of the Giants" is enclosed by towering volcanic peaks and is filled with these strange rocky forms chiseled by Nature's hand. Elephants, gigantic frogs, walruses and dinosauria seem to appear in great troops. The Tuareg firmly believe that they are the evil spirits of enemies turned into stone as they sought escape from the wrathful, avenging hand of their ancestors.

---

1.   "Shame enters the family that tills the soil." Tuareg Proverb.

The camp was set amidst these weird surroundings, and while dinner was being prepared we played our powerful motor searchlights over these fantastic rock formations. The startling effect caused no little wonder and amusement, especially among the younger Tuareg.

On the second day in this camp we tested the athletic powers of these superbly magnificent physical specimens. We had running and jumping and javelin throwing – a sort of Olympic games of the Sahara! We had heard so much of their physical prowess that we were in some measure prepared for the startling results of our games. Several – not one – cleared the bar at six feet, running straight at the jump. What they could do if well trained is impossible to forecast, but certain it is that many college coaches would glow with enthusiasm at the prospect of having one of these Tuareg youths on his track team.

The standing broad jump is one of their great events. Although a fair performer myself, they outclassed me in the high jump, the broad jump, and races at all distances, and their time was not far short of Olympic records – untrained, barefooted, and running on sand! I suggested to one of the officers of the Southern Territories that a team should represent the Tuareg at the next Olympic games, and if this should be brought about, I feel certain that such performers as Nurmi and Ritola would get a great shock at the speed and endurance of these sons of the endless spaces.

El Quaff, whom I saw win the last classic Marathon in 1928, was a blood cousin of the Tuareg. They are splendid wrestlers, despite the fact that even in this vigorous sport the ever present veil is worn. It must be remembered that the Tuareg never removes his veil in the presence of others, and no man, even a blood brother, ever looks on his face. Should the veil come loose, or be torn from his face by some unhappy accident, the Tuareg would hurry for the seclusion of a sheltering rock, or duck behind his camel, where he could readjust this highly important piece of wearing apparel. I wondered, as I watched them wrestling, what would happen if one of them should have the ill fortune to lose his veil. I feel certain that his antagonist would instantly cease all efforts until the embarrassed one could return to the game more suitably clothed!

Interesting as were all their games, and surprising as were the results, the one mental picture that I shall always retain is the memory of their Greek-like torsos when, stripped to the waist and ready for their sports, they stood like so many classic statues, silhouetted on "the roof of the Sahara."

Tuareg endurance is the subject of many a desert camp fire tale, and it is common knowledge that he completes many a journey after his camel has fallen by the way. His camels are his main possession, and they are his faithful companions through life. He is born by the camel's side; he remains by him until death. The Hoggar camel is a magnificent beast, with a thick, shaggy coat, and is far taller than the ordinary camel. He is truly a fit companion for the Tuareg.

It is uncertain when the camel was first introduced into the Sahara. Some historians put it as late as the fourth century, A. D., but I feel that it was much earlier than this. Indeed, I cannot imagine the Tuareg ever having existed without his useful and inseparable companion, the Hoggar camel. It is said that ancient desert transportation was carried on by means of oxen.[1] The oxen of the ancient Garamantians are depicted on several of the rock sculptures of the Sahara, crude drawings which were first seen by Barth on the rocks of Telizzarhen in the heart of the desert.

But to-day the Tuareg travels by camel – or on foot if disaster places him in such predicament. With a little water in a skin, a bag of dates for food, he is off! – ready for hundreds of miles.

---

1.   Herodotus IV, p. 183.

The chief pastime of the veiled ones is the sport of raiding. As soon as the Tuareg is old enough to ride a camel his one ambition is to raid, and he finds ready teachers to assist him in the realization of his dreams. Distances are nothing to these pirates of the sands. They have been known to ride, when forced, a hundred miles in a day, but as a rule they do about forty miles and this, considering the nature of the terrain, is indeed a good average.

The early training of the Tuareg youth is Spartan-like in its severity. From the day a Tuareg boy takes the veil (at about the age of fifteen) he is considered to have come into man's estate. Then, proceeding on the theory that he is made of iron, his elders no longer make the way easy for him. He can go four or five days without water, and can go without food for more than a week. Such denial, to all appearances, in no way lessens his physical stamina, and it is certain that it places no drain upon his resolute spirit. Perhaps this can be accounted for in some measure by the fact that he is generally half starved, is all muscle and brawn, and has not the slightest chance to become obese. He is always dieting – involuntarily.

A Tuareg has been known to travel a thousand kilometers (over six hundred miles) on foot, carrying his water and food on his back! It is due to their unequaled endurance and stoical indifference to hardship and suffering that they have been dreaded since time immemorial by all the other races of Africa.

Their raids are swift and sudden. As a rule they attack a camp at dawn; there follows a hand to hand fight of unbelievable intensity and vigor and they are gone, rapidly diminishing specks on the boundless horizon. They will raid an oasis camp or caravan a thousand miles from the scene of the planning and then retire into their mountain fastness where they will "be low" for months.

Many are the caves hidden in the great Hoggar Mountains still filled with the fruits of raids conducted hundreds of years ago, and that is why every now and then we come across Seventeenth Century guns, and coins of the Middle Ages! C. Killian found such a cave in 1921[1] and the King of the Hoggar told me that he knew where several treasure troves were located – but that is all I could get him to tell.

While among the Tuareg camps in the Hoggar I noticed that some of the camps were far away from water wells and that they had to transport their water for many miles. My questions in this direction brought forth the answer that they never camp near water for fear of a raid, as raiders always make for water points in hope of finding a camp or caravan.

To go back for a moment to the question of Tuareg endurance, I will cite the now famous case of the super-Marathon runner of Agades who, in 1916, rode and ran a distance of two hundred and fifty miles in three days to seek relief for the sorely besieged French garrison of Agades. This heroic man carried the message of life and death to the commander of the troops at Zinder, falling dead at the feet of the commandant, but not until he had fought back death long enough to gasp out his appeal for relief.[2]

To-day his grave is marked by the laconic MORT POUR LA FRANCE, yet his memory should live with those of the heroes of old.

The Tuareg is supremely indifferent to the rapid changes in temperature common to the Central Sahara. Whenever I think of that camp in the "Valley of the Giants" it is to recall the shivering cold nights and the sturdy Tuareg who sleep "as they are," wearing the same garments they wore in the day, despite the fact that there is a difference of 70 degrees in temperature. He has excellent reasons for retiring fully clothed, for his life is a life of preparedness. He is ready to take the trail the moment he arises

---

1.   *Au Hoggar,* C. Killian, *1921.*
2.   Siege of Agades, 1916. This episode has been handled in fiction. See *Beau Geste.*

or what is more to the point, he is "booted and spurred and armed for the fray." In short, he is a superb child of the desert, to whom the desert belongs.[1] He alone knows her moods, her caprices, her heartless buffetings, and he alone is her equal!

The Royal Encampment in the Heart of the Hoggar

For the purposes of this work it will not be necessary to involve the reader in all the phases of the controversy raging around the question of the origin of the Tuareg, but it may be well to point out the various theories and they are yet little more than theories. The general opinion held by the greater number of students is that "The People of the Veil" are a part of the great Berber race of North Africa. However, there are scholars of distinction who hold the opinion that the Tuareg is of Libyan-Semitic origin and came from the East. Still others have thought them to be early Christians driven southward after the death at Carthage of that idealistic crusader, St. Louis, or the remnant of the terrible Donatist Schism that with fire and sword laid waste all of North Africa. Again, they may be the descendants of the Carthaginians, of Byzantium, or of the Vandals, all of whom conquered North Africa.

There is still a great study ahead on this subject. Suffice it to be known that this once great race is of white origin, has many peculiarities of its own and is of great age, as the tomb of Queen Tin Hinan proved. Only by continuing the great work of exploring the mountains of the Hoggar, Air and Tibesti may we hope to solve the problems of Tuareg origin.

It was this ever present hope of learning something more of these people that led me, while at the camp in the "Valley

---

1. The last words spoken to me by the King of the Hoggar were, "And don't forget, the Sahara belongs to us!"

of the Giants," to arrange for a visit to the Royal Encampment of the King of the Hoggar. Observing, therefore, their own customs in such matters, we sent ahead certain presents which served far better than words to properly introduce us and assure us of a welcome. Tuaregs do not, as a rule, extend hearty welcome to strangers, but we could hardly ask for better treatment than we received at the hands of the famous Kel Reli, the noblest of the Tuareg tribes living in the Hoggar. There, as guests of the king, Akhamouk, we lived under their tents and learned many secrets of their lives. Through the courtesies of this king we took the first motion pictures of Tuareg life, using up forty thousand feet of film! That is a rather staggering footage, but we filmed in detail all the interesting phases of their lives.

It was in the Royal Encampment that I first had the certainty that the legendary Queen Tin Hinan was something more than a legend and that it was the Tuareg belief that she was buried in the mausoleum of Abelessa. It came about in this fashion: Tuareg history is largely a matter of legendary tales, kept alive and current by a tribal story-teller. He has, literally, a "bag of tales." The bag of tales consists of a skin pouch filled with small round pebbles, very much alike to the inexperienced eye, but to the keeper thereof each pebble represents a story. These stories are told in the order in which the pebbles are withdrawn from the bag.

The story-teller at the Royal Encampment came to entertain me with his "bag of tales," and, to my unbounded joy, told me the details of Queen Tin Hinan and of Takamat, her slave. So graphic was his tale, and so well did it bear out the fragments of other legends, that I was fired with a new enthusiasm to locate her sepulchre. This find is treated in detail in another chapter of this book,[1] but I may say here that I still have and prize the Tuareg "bag of tales" which

---

1.   See Chapter 5, "The Discovery of the Tomb of Queen Tin Hinan."

unlocked for me a secret hidden for centuries by the silences of the desert.

Our life among the Tuareg at their encampment was very pleasant. Slowly we gained their confidence and friendship. Due to the efforts of our splendid interpreters. Belaid and Chapuis, we spent many evenings listening to their legends, and in making a careful study of their customs. For the sake of clarity it may be wise to treat their customs, arts, and legends under separate headings, and with this in mind we will turn first to:

The Veil

The Tuareg noble is never without his veil. Night and day, sleeping, eating, traveling or fighting, the veil is never removed. Many theories have been advanced concerning the reason for the wearing of the veil. Some have thought it to be a form of disguise, such as has ever been worn by bandits; others have thought it to be a protection against the sand and wind; still others claim that it has been handed down from the period when the negro empires swept over the Sahara and the Tuareg, being in the minority, put on the black veil in order to pass as negroes and thus escape death. As a matter of fact, the veil must be a part of the Tuareg's religion or cult.[1] He himself knows little or nothing of its origin. For him it is enough to know that it has been handed down from generation to generation.

The effect of seeing all the tall, veiled, silent men is quite inspiring, even though a bit frightening. The dark blue and black veils lend an air of mystery and I have always felt that they serve to create an atmosphere of strong animosity.

Strange as it may seem, the Tuareg women are never veiled, nor do they paint their faces. It is the braves who

---

1. It may well have come from the ceremonies surrounding the cult of the veil of Tanit.

make use of the veil and who paint that portion of their faces showing above the veil.

As earlier stated, the Tuareg youth "takes the veil" when he is about fifteen years of age. We filmed this strange ceremony as well as the ceremony of the sword. The sword is the symbol of chivalry, as were spurs in the Middle Ages.

It is interesting to note that the Tuareg have many symbols which would seem to connect them with the period of the early Crusades. The Roman cross is an emblem quite common among them, though they know little or nothing of the story of the Christ and are lukewarm Mohammedans.

I have earlier mentioned the fact that they hold knightly tournaments and their two-handed swords and shields bear strong resemblance to the arms common to the day "When Knighthood Was in Flower."

Again I am digressing, but it is not easy to always keep to the subject matter. Whatever the origin of the veil it is certain that it has been a great protection to the Tuareg raiders, for, of course, so masked they are unrecognizable and have again and again escaped punishment because no accuser could point his finger at any one of them and be sure of the identification.

The Libyan Script

Second in interest to the wearing of the veil is the survival of the ancient Libyan script among the Tuareg people. They still use the ancient writing of their ancestors. Scholars have declared that it shows traces of Phoenician and Mediterranean origin, but I see no reason to believe that it had its origin outside of Africa. In centuries past the Tuareg had a far higher degree of civilization than at present. This was definitely established in the discovery of Queen Tin Hinan's tomb.

In the Hoggar I have often watched the Tuareg women writing on the rocks, sometimes from right to left, sometimes from left to right and sometimes up and down. The rocks of the Sahara are covered with this strange script you see it from Morocco to Siwa, and from Tunisia to Timbuktu – names, declarations of love, rendezvous, poetry and child-like messages. It is one of the romances and mysteries of the desert.

Poetry and Social Customs

The Tuareg are born poets. To have been present at one of their "Ahals" is a never- to- be- forgotten experience. The women are especially given to the development of poetry and its preservation. While visiting the Royal Encampment we were fortunate enough to obtain all the new poems of the celebrated poetess Dassine, and her "Poems of the Hoggar" is one of my treasured books.

The "Ahal," a strange social meeting, provides the Tuareg poet and poetess with an opportunity of presenting to the world their newest poems. Perhaps it would be better to say that the "Ahal" is something more than a social gathering – it is a literary meeting at which all the Tuareg literati gather to recite their war odes, their historic and legendary poems, and to test their wits in sharp repartee with the educated and noble women of the tribe. An invitation to an "Ahal" will bring Tuareg nobles from hundreds of miles. It seems that in the Hoggar, as elsewhere in the world, poets will travel a long way for the privilege of reciting their newest odes.

The "Ahal" is always held at night, and as a rule during the more seasonable part of the year. The tents of the ladies are first pitched in a large circle, and it is to the center of this circle that the nobles come. The early part of the night will be taken up by the recitation of poems and odes. Toward morning, however, the literary flavoring of the gathering passes away and the "Ahal" becomes an orgy but perhaps it is too much to expect even a poet to continue rhyming all the night long.

At this meeting in the desert "salon" the poems are often accompanied by a musical instrument called the Amzad. Imagine these intellectuals of the Sahara coming from all parts of the desert to listen to beautiful love and war ballads, accompanied by plaintive, haunting melodies.

Some of the hostesses are really *grandes dames,* refined, intelligent and dignified. Though the art of repartee may be losing ground in the civilized world, it is still very much alive in this part of "Darkest Africa." It is true that these children of the desert are free with their sentiments and feelings, but their actions are so natural that it fails to be shocking. Often when in the toil and fret of modern life, I thankfully look back upon some of those silver-starred nights in the Sahara when the knights and ladies of the Tuareg tribe gathered around their camp fire and music, love and ballads became the order of the magic hour.

Dancing is nearly unknown to these "People of the Veil." It is too undignified for the stately nobles of the desert; they are too proud to hop around to the beating of drums, as is done in the uncivilized negro empires of the southland. Let us hope that the "Ahal" shall continue unspoiled by any modern influences and that these romantic meetings under the stars shall continue until the end of time.

It might be well to give here some examples of the poetic expressions of the Tuareg nobles. It will be noticed that their themes, in keeping with their lives, are of battles and of valiant deeds. The first example is from Songs of the Hoggar, by the Tuareg poetess, Dassine, and was taken down at an "Ahal" by Sergeant Belaid Mohamed Ben Ali, the official guide of our expedition into the Hoggar.

"To all those who assemble at your 'love meeting', to those of this land, to those that live in far off d'Tkha-men-Khamen, and particularly to you, Dassine, I send this proclamation:

"Whenever the cowards that hid from the battle, and are trying to hide near you, are seen, curse these cow-ards! We saw them the day we fought with the enemy. There was a great battle with powder and balls, and so many javelins were thrown that the sky became as a tent of steel.

"When the enemy fled I drew my sword and their limbs fell about like the cut off branches of the jerjir. . ."

The next example is the Lament of Moussa-ag-Amastan, Amenokal of the Hoggar, and is also for Dassine, the famed Tuareg poetess.

"Like thou, O Dassine-oult-Yemma, death in battle has preferred others than I, and for the lion's share has cho-sen Djelloul, whose head was broken by a club. Mechegdi, blinded by a dagger, seeks in his madness to find the sun. Ebeggi, whose heart was opened by a scimiter as an orange is opened with a knife; Akelaoui, whose entrails lay like red serpents in the sand; Boulk-adjmi, nailed to the sands by spears, two through the hands and two through the feet and whose belly became swollen like a rounded shield in the sun."

"And I cried at the enemy, who thought he had gained the victory – 'Avaunt, impure ones! Infidels unfaithful to your sworn faith! Mokhazens of the Tell and Sahel, bought brigands, slaves of gold, in your dark coverings

of dishonor you are but children of Death, sons of owls and of the night.'

"By the burst open head of Djelloul, by the hanging entrails of Akelaoui, like those of a cut open ram, I shall charge at you to avenge them, and swifter than the lightning my sword shall kill you! "And my fame shall, perhaps, make me beloved by Dassine-oult-Yemma, the most lovely."

Whether the Amenokal (king) made good on his boast, I cannot say, but his compliment to Dassine, the poetess, would serve to insure its wide reading.

The third example is the war song of a Tuareg noble. It is not as defiant as the King's lament, but it serves as a testament to the warrior's courage in battle and in defeat.

"And I tell ye, O reasonable women, and those who paint your lips and nostrils, and thou who presideth:

"At Amessera, near Tit, we mutually made battle with javelins, pagan guns, and the broadsword. I smote the enemy and was wounded in return until, like a purple mantle, I was covered in blood from the shoulders to the ends of my arms.

"The young women, who sit at the Ahal, will never hear it said that I hid behind the rocks! Three times I was picked up, fainting and insensible. They tied me with cords to a Mehari. But defeat is not dishonor, for against the Prophet himself the pagans won victory in the days of old. . ."

The Little Queens (Tamenoukhalen)

Such is the beautiful name which the chivalrous Tuareg husbands and lovers give to the Tuareg women. The first thing that strikes one in a study of these people is the high status of the women. Chivalry is not dead among the men of the tribe and the women hold a unique position in this hidden corner of the world. This position of power and influence is a direct hold-over from antiquity, for since earliest time women have held an exalted position among the Libyan civilizations. At Carthage they worshiped the strange and terrible divinity called Tanit, to whom countless children were offered up in dreadful sacrifice. Even the name "Libyan" comes from a female deity called "Libya." Queen Tin Hinan was a historic personage – the Eve of the Sahara[1] from whom all the noble Tuaregs claim descent. The Goddess Athena, and the famed Amazon[2] of mythology probably originated in Africa, and it is said that Helen of Troy[3] disappeared "into the heart of Libya." The last of the Amazons still engage in warfare and to this day handle the affairs of state.

Survivals of the matriarchal are numerous among the Tuaregs. The female never veils her face, is entirely independent in her actions, has complete authority over the home and the rearing of the children, owns property and goods in her own name, and chooses and courts her future husband. The Tuareg nobles revere their women and each has only one wife. "We are neither negroes nor heathen," they stoutly declare, "and, therefore, a Tuareg has only one wife."[4] (Civilized world please copy.)

I shall never forget the graceful and proud bearing of the women in the camp of King Akhamouk. Especially do I

---

1. Ben Hazra, *Six mois chez les Toureg Ahaggar.*
2. Diodorus Siculus, and S. Gsell.
3. Pindar, and Herodotus.
4. Gautier, *Essai de Phychologie Colonial.*

recall the friendly queen and her court, the intellectual Dassine, poet laureate of her beloved desert people, the *grandes
dames,* Tehit Oult Chedab, Dachi Oult El Martar, R'zzahra
Oult Souri, and half a dozen other elegant and sparkling
ladies.

Several Tuareg girls whom I saw at Tamanrasset, In
Salah, and in different desert camps, were quite pretty, full
of laughter and jokes and with an unaffected, simple friendship that was a pleasure to witness.

Since the days of La Kahena the bravery of the Tuareg
women is proverbial throughout Africa. In a battle fought
not long ago, the women of Kel Fade led the Tuareg nobles
into the fighting line, interposing their own bodies between
their husbands and the enemy, thus preventing the French
from firing. Mr. Rodd tells of a modern Amazon in the
heroic person of Barkasho of the Ikazkazam, who led raids
and waged battle with the enemies of her people. Like Joan
of Arc she bore the armor of a man. She adopted the veil and
sword of the male, and made her name famous throughout
the land, but in the end she returned to her home and household occupation.[1]

The Tuareg girl dresses quite simply in dark garments
wrapped around her body, beginning under the armpits, with
one end of the garment brought over the shoulder. Ordinarily
they wear little jewelry and the men wear none at all. The
slaves of the women do most of the work. The men are more
skilled in the art of sewing than the women and are able to
cook and tidy up the household. These practices are not, of
course, regarded as effeminate.

The Tuareg girl finding herself in love will ride great distances to visit the object of her affections and will return to
her own camp at dawn. In this upside down land the woman
proposes to the man – and thus "the female of the species is
more deadly than the male." In earlier days it was a custom
for the Tuareg noble to offer his wife to whoever paid him a

1.   Jean, C., *Le Touareg du Sud-Est* and F. R. Rodd in *People of the Veil*, p. 171.

visit, considering this a sign of courteous welcome. If the visitor declined, the noble was deeply offended and considered it as uncomplimentary to the beauty of the lady in question. But this is no longer the custom at least, none of the members of our party faced any such uncomfortable experience.

The women of the Hoggar still sleep on the tombs of their ancestors when they wish to consult the future. Their thought is that while sleeping on the tomb a vision will come to them and they will be able to peep into the future. A Tuareg maiden, in love, will spend the night on the tomb of some ancestor with the hope of catching a vision of her lover who is away at war or on a raid.

We took some interesting films of Tuareg girls lying on old tombs. We also witnessed and filmed the modest way in which the Tuareg ladies meet strangers. They first group themselves in the distance, then slowly advance in a zigzag way so that the men may be given time to prepare for their arrival. They never lose their dignity, never forget their noble ancestors and never become familiar. As Mr. Rodd remarks, "the little girls are beautifully reserved and respectful, especially to their parents." The Tuareg have many virtues which we might copy. Marauders and desert pirates though they be, they still command respect for certain of these virtues.

I shall never forget the tournament which was staged for us but which was announced as being given *in honor of the ladies.* There was jousting and sword play; there were feats of arms that would have done justice to any knight of old. And as we looked on we could but recall the days of King Arthur and his noble knights. It is strange to see here in the desert the sign of the cross on shields, swords and saddles. It is indeed reminiscent of the Crusaders, from whom not a few students think the Tuareg is descended. It is a romantic thought, but I fear it is far from the fact. True, they have a noble origin, and a mediaeval code of chivalry. They bear the sign of the cross emblazoned on their shields and weapons; they carry the crusader-like, double-handed sword, and their knightly tournaments bear a great resemblance to those held on the Continent ten centuries ago.

In this connection it will be well to remember that St. Louis of France on his last crusade died amidst his knights in the ruins of Carthage in 1270. With this fact in mind, some scholars believe that these Tuareg nobles are descendants of those Crusaders. Certainly there are evidences in support of the thought, but one must not forget the overwhelming mass of evidence to the contrary. There is the survival of the Libyan Script to be considered; there are Tuareg tombs of greater antiquity than the day of St. Louis of France; there are inscriptions on the rocks that were ancient when St. Louis was born. It would be safer to hazard the guess that certain customs of the Crusaders were copied by the Tuareg, customs which were made to order for the fighting marauders of the desert.

It will be a long time before we will solve the mysteries surrounding these fascinating people. In their land are many deep, unexplored canyons; lost oases surrounded by the awful Tanezrouft, where Tuareg tell me there are two ruined cities, Tokalet and Tafassaset; and still awaiting discovery are the emerald mines of the Garamantians, from whence came the jewels found in Queen Tin Hinan's tomb.

The land of the Tuareg is a rich storehouse of knowledge for future explorers. If ever the cradle of man is discovered and proven, it is my belief that it will be here in the Sahara. But it will take long, patient toil and it will come as the fruit of an expedition equipped for years of work in this land so difficult of access, and where students and explorers are still subjected to hostile raids and massacres.

If the eyes of scientists could only behold what the eyes of the Tuareg have beheld, then our fund of knowledge would be multiplied a thousand fold. But the desert is the Tuareg's home. He finds comfort where we find hardship; he walks fearlessly where we go with fear; he can outfit himself in an hour for a long trail for which we would make weeks of preparation; he conquers the desert – we only explore it.

Physical Aspects of the Hoggar

The Hoggar, the wild and romantic land of the Tuareg, is, apart from Tibesti, the most mountainous region of the Sahara. The center of this stronghold of the "Knights of the Desert" is called by them the Atakor N'Ahaggar, and is the headquarters of the Tobol or Tuareg Confederation.

The massif is of crystalline formation and is of recent volcanic origin, of magnificent aspect. Legends and desert superstitions have lent a halo of awe and mystery to this nearly inaccessible mass of beetling crags, frowning precipices and foreboding, spirit-haunted canyons.

The climate is dry and sparkling, a combination of the clear, transparent atmosphere of the desert and the invigorating, limpid, tonic-like air of the Alps. The heat is dry and one feels it far less than the humid atmosphere of the seaside. One seems never to tire in the Hoggar.

The vegetation is sparse, the upper slopes of the mountains are denuded of the plant life which is found only in the river beds and near the wells that reach to the great subterranean lakes of the Sahara. The most important and most numerous trees are the Ethel, which give a large spread of shade, a Godsend to the weary traveler in the heat of the day. The Talha and the Tamat, and other acacia trees, sometimes form magnificent groups of greenery, a vivid contrast to the glistening black and gray of the dead volcanoes. Despite the sparseness of the plant life, the bareness of the land does not give one the feeling of melancholy; on the contrary, the vast masses of rock, the endless silent plains, and the bold outlines of the needle-like peaks, give one the feeling of repose and majestic calm.

Perhaps the very strangeness of the land itself has had its influence upon the inhabitants thereof, for to me the Tuareg always appeared like strange apparitions riding on giant white camels, their faces hidden behind their veils and seeming to glide down the gloomy canyons in a manner that makes them ghostlike and utterly unreal.

The Tuareg are a tall race of people, nearly all six-footers. In their flowing garments, and with eyes gleaming above their veils, they are the living pictures of our youth-imagined giants. They are beautiful specimens – Greek mountain gods. Very few of them are stout. Before we had met the King of the Tuareg, one of the tribesmen said, "If you meet a fat man, you can be certain that it is the Amenokal." The women are well formed and wear graceful, enveloping robes, bound tightly under the arms. They have a proud way of walking that brings to the mind the goddesses of ancient Greece. Perhaps, after all, they are the last of the Atlanteans.

I have never seen such beautiful hands and delicate feet as those of the nobles of the Hoggar, nor can one forget the beauty of their large, solemn eyes. The expression "as graceful as a gazelle" seems appropriate to the Tuareg girl and I shall never forget the rippling sparkle of their laughter.

How the Tuareg enjoys a joke! His laugh is spontaneous and hearty, and he laughs often and long. It is difficult to imagine a gayer lot than a group of Tuareg boys and girls joking with each other. These same people are the ones who killed Flatters and holy Pere de Foucauld, a people of many moods and terrible in revenge. I heard of a Tuareg whose wife had been carried off in a raid and his two sons killed. He waited his hour and, though the desert is vast, never gave up hope in his seemingly endless search. At last he found the murderer and buried him, alive, up to the neck, near a large ant hill. Next morning only a white, grinning skull remained as testament to the fierceness of Tuareg revenge.

The Tuareg are divided into three classes: the nobles, the serfs, and the servants or slaves. As in feudal times, the serfs pay tribute to the lords and nobles. When the noble visits the camp of his vassal, his children, camels and his entire retinue are provided with food and shelter. Be it said to their credit, however, that the nobles do not take advantage of these rights. The nobles are the directors of the Confederation. They plan the raids, the caravan treks, arrange for the protection of the camps and plan the wars. The women take a great part in the social and political tribal structure.

The sign of noble dignity is a great drum, the Tobol. We took a marvelous film of the King having the Tobol beaten to assemble the tribe. The drum is so constructed as to be held by one hand while it is beaten with a stick on which is a ball of leather. The sound of the drumming can be heard for many, many miles, and it is a marvelous spectacle to see the tribesmen assemble at the sound of the drum. From mountain and dale they come, flying over the desert on their giant, racing Mehari camels, garments and veils fluttering in the wind and long rifles held high as they race for the tent of the Amenokal.

While in the Hoggar we saw three noble tribes grouped around their various chieftains, but all of them recognized the Amenokal as their supreme chief. The Berber is generally a fiercely independent individual, and it seems strange that the Tuareg should have a feudal system. No Tuareg noble ever works, the negroes and slaves do all the work.

The entire population of the Hoggar is about five thousand souls. Attempts have been made to introduce agriculture – a futile effort to change their raiding tendencies. They are nomads and will always remain so. During the past twenty-five years, France has somewhat pacified the fierce Hoggar tribesmen, but they are always looking back to the good old days when they raided from one end of the Sahara to the other to their heart's content. They remind me of retired pirates, forced to sit around their camp fires, dreaming of the freebooting days of old. I asked a group of them if they would like to go raiding again. Their answer was a heavy sigh that came from the heart.

The old fellows are now surrounded by the envious and slightly more peaceful new generation, relating to them feats of war and pillage. "Those were the grand days," they say at the end of some reminiscence dealing with sudden raid and death. They glance fondly at their guns and daggers, and then with longing look away to the far, far horizon. In many ways this ancient white race is a truly remarkable people.

They are now making their last stand against extinction amid their beloved mountains. The Tuareg, last descendants of the once mighty Libyan peoples, are dying out as fast as civilization reaches them. Like the American Indians, they will soon be but a romantic legend. They have changed greatly in the past two generations. Their enforced peaceful living has smothered the old fires of initiative and energy.

The caravan trading is disappearing – the end of slavery dealt that trade its death blow. Soon the automobile and Trans-Saharan Railway and the irrigation of certain large depressions will change the Sahara.

Then new pages in its history will begin. As a result, the tribesmen will be driven still further back until at last they will disappear under the wave of civilization. Old trails are fading. Ancient camping grounds are silent and melancholy. Soon the long caravan of the Veiled Ones will have passed into the night.

Farewell, brave souls! You have been my good friends, loyal and sincere. Your veils hid from me your faces, but I saw the sincerity in your eyes. Yours is a tragic destiny, but for you there must be new happy raiding grounds. You, like your Western brothers, the American Indians, are moving toward the vast free horizons of the Great Beyond. Soon you must pass to your Islands of the Blessed, to your dream of Land of the Hereafter. . .

Chapter 5

THE TOMB OF QUEEN TIN HINAN

"The Worldly Hope men set their hearts upon
Turns Ashes – or it prospers; and anon
Like Snow upon the Desert's dusty face,
Lighting a little hour or two – was gone."
                                    – Omar Khayyam.

The ancient world abounds with legends that are closely allied with facts, and it is highly important when one is hunting for a lost city, oasis, or tomb, to follow up what the natives have to say in regard to the stories of great treasures, superstitions and legends. In the foregoing chapter, mention was made of the Tuareg story-teller who " let the cat out of the bag," and then told me enough concerning the famous Queen Tin Hinan to convince me that legend could be changed to fact. It was through the development of this story that I made what is considered one of the greatest archaeological discoveries in the history of the Sahara – the finding of the tomb of Queen Tin Hinan.

Of course, it took months of organization, as well as studious research into the ancient chronicles, stories, legends and accounts of the wild desert tribes. The minutiae of such preparations are of little interest to the average reader, but you can be sure it was an exciting moment when, after two weeks of continual travel across the desert, we saw at last the great edifice of the semi-legendary queen. Queen Tin

Hinan is the historic ancestor of all the great Tuareg confederation, and her sepulchre is situated on the east bank of the
dried-out bed of the Abelessa River.

Chudeau, the French savant, claims that Tin Hinan is as
historic a figure as Jugurtha, Koceila, La Kahena, and the
other great Berber heroes. The date of Queen Tin Hinan's
life has now been solved by the information gained during
the examination of the matter taken from her tomb. This
information has given us the earliest known Tuareg historical date, and we are now slowly building up a more definite
history of these people, whose past is so difficult to ascer-
tain, due to the strong Tuareg custom forbidding one to
speak of the dead. "The dead once buried are best left
alone," says the Tuareg, and perhaps this provides us with
the reason why the Veiled Ones seem to have no veneration
or cult of the dead, and early tombs are, in consequence,
very difficult to find.

While visiting the royal encampment of the Tuareg, as
recounted in the preceding chapter, Akhamouk, the
Amenokal (king) of the Tuareg spoke to me at length of
these people and their history. "We have always been nobles,
warriors, and poets," he said proudly. "We have always been
mighty and powerful, and in the past ruled all the Sahara."

Since childhood Amenokal Akhamouk had been taught
to hate the Arabs, the last of the great invaders, and to look
upon them more or less as negroes. Certainly he regards
them as an inferior race. The Tuareg has always defeated the
Arab in battle. On any fair field, one Tuareg is worth half a
dozen Arabs.

The present enemy of the Tuareg are the French, but the
old king hid his feelings from me regarding his opinion of
their domination. He did say, however, that the Battle of Tit,
in 1904, was the reason why some of the Hoggar nobles
fought against France in the World War. At the battle of Tit
(previously mentioned in Chapter 1) a hundred and twenty

nobles fell. The modern machine guns triumphed over spears and shields.

In the chapter dealing with Tuareg customs, I have outlined the high position held by the women. This custom of holding the woman supreme must go as far back as the time of Queen Tin Hinan, and in some measure accounts for the endurance of the legends concerning her. In our own history we have some striking examples of the power of the fair sex in the matter of leadership – Queen Elizabeth, Queen Anne, Catherine of Russia, Joan of Arc, Isabel of Spain, and the Victoria of our days. In Africa we find a still longer list of female leaders who stamped themselves upon the history and the religion of that country.

Tanit, the supreme divinity of North Africa, was certainly of Berber origin. She is not a Phoenician Goddess, and existed a thousand years before Christ, when the Tyrians and Sidonians first made their colonies on the coast of Libya. (Libya is the ancient name of this land, mentioned historically on Egyptian monuments at least fifteen hundred years before Christ.) Tanit was also a familiar divinity or queen, and I have often wondered if Tin Hinan were not another name for Libya or Tanit.[1]

From the Tuareg I have learned that Queen Tin Hinan lived at the time when the Tuareg empire reached from the Atlantic to the Nile. It would seem that the Tuareg, or Berber, came from the north, and may have been driven south by the Carthaginians and Romans. By a strange discovery made several weeks after our return from the expedition to Queen Tin Hinan's tomb, we definitely placed the date of her reign. While cleaning up the many articles of the treasure, we found, in a sculptured wooden bowl, four gold coins bearing the effigy of the Emperor Constantine.[2] These coins had been buried with her.

1. Prorok – Annual Report Smithsonian Institute – "Temple of Tanit."

2. Kelsey – *Excavations at Carthage*, 1926. Prorok – *Art and Archaeology*. Gsell – *Tombeau de Tin Hinan*, Paris, 1927.

It is possible, of course, that they antedated her death, or even the beginning of her reign, but when we delve back into so dim a past we must content ourselves with something less than the accuracy of dates with which we are so familiar in our everyday modern life. After all, our purpose was not to discover the birthday of Queen Tin Hinan, or to interview someone "who knew her when," but to separate her from the maze of past centuries, and in so doing find her influence upon the development of the customs, the life, and the glories of her people.

The tomb of this legendary mother of all the Tuareg was on a small eminence of rock overlooking the Oed Abelessa. The first view – a mass of stone crowning a hill – is had from a considerable distance. As soon as we reached the base of the ruin, we were amazed at the proportions of the edifice, and wondered what manner of men and which civilization could have built such a magnificent and enduring monument in the heart of the Sahara.

Imagine, if you will, the thrill that came to us on finding here in the heart of the mountains, a hundred miles south of the Hoggar, an edifice which on first view appeared as grand as one of the smaller pyramids. After this came the quickening thought that somewhere under those stones might be found the crypt of the famous Queen Tin Hinan, surrounded by her nobles and bedecked in jewels of earliest antiquity. These quickening thoughts account for the eagerness with which we made ready to prosecute our search.

As soon as our camp was set we went in search of the Caid of a nearby negro village, beginning our explorations by unearthing that dignitary. This is not a figure of speech, for his home was actually below the surface of the earth. We placed before him our official demand for men. After the usual and customary heated discussions, he succeeded in mustering about twenty-five fairly presentable specimens, although we had asked for fifty.

Our first problem was how to approach the edifice, the stone being piled up in such a formidable way that for a while it appeared we would have to attack the monument by siege, and in some fashion effect a breach in the wall. I was resolved to start a passage to the central and high point of the edifice. Soon we were hard at work moving great blocks of stone, which were cut quite regular and from three to four feet in length. The outside wall is of splendid workmanship and resembles in design the "Tomb of the Christian," and the Medracin, those two great Berber monuments of Algeria, one of which contains the tomb of Juba II, the other containing the bodies of Cleopatra Celene, and her husband. Celene, it will be remembered, was the gifted daughter of Cleopatra and Anthony.

In examining the stones of the great exterior wall, we found, to our amazement, that many of the stones were covered with thousands of inscriptions. Some of these were undoubtedly ancient, others were more modern, and many of them were recent love messages of passing lovelorn Tuareg tribesmen. There is a legend among the Tuareg to the effect that whoever inscribes a wish, or a vow, on the stones of the great tomb, will most certainly have the wish granted, or the vow eternalized.

It is the custom of these veiled people to be completely unveiled in the affairs of the heart, and both men and women inscribe on every suitable rock their innermost feelings, boldly attaching their names thereto. This custom will doubtless disappear on the very day when breach of promise suits are introduced to the Sahara.

Many of the inscriptions uncovered in the process of taking down the exterior wall were of great antiquity, the letters burned black by a thousand thousand suns. The great structure itself is surrounded by a dozen tombs, built in a circle, and on an artificial platform of stones. We started excavating these, as well as the central monument, thinking them to be a part of the whole ensemble. Later, however, we discovered that they were the last resting places of the twelve noble followers of the Queen.[1]

As our excavations progressed we were struck by the beautiful arrangement of the stone walls which divided the edifice into twelve rooms, the stones being well joined. The outside wall we excavated to a depth of twenty feet. Its thickness at the summit being five feet, at the base nearly twenty feet, and the entire wall rises forty feet above the foundation. Most of the rooms measured from six to eight yards square. Leading from the northeast we found the sculptured ruin of a large entrance, the door thereto being covered by a large stone upon which were many ancient inscriptions. On either side of the main passage were regularly placed pillars of volcanic stone, beautifully worked, and leading toward the central room.

As the work went forward it became more evident that we were excavating an edifice that was something more than a tomb – it must have been some sacred temple. We knew that legend, semi-historical in nature, placed the tomb of the great queen here, but it is possible that, after her reign and death, a cult found its origin on the site to which so many pilgrimages were made by all those who worshiped the memory of Queen Tin Hinan. Or, perhaps, they may have worshiped some now unknown divinity.

On the third day of our work, after excavating six feet of rock and sand, we came upon the remains of the storeroom. Here we found many date pits, millet, and a considerable quantity of vegetable matter. We found here, also, some iridescent glass.

The work was very laborious, long, and slow. It was necessary for the stones to be removed by the none too eager negroes, who passed them from hand to hand. All stones, upon which inscriptions appeared, were put aside for the day

---

1. Embedded in the rocks at the base of the tomb we found many inscriptions and symbols impossible to decipher. It is maddening to think that here may be an enlightening page of lost history.

when a Libyan language expert can decipher them, and this scholar will then add greatly to our present fund of information. He will have a field worthy of his efforts, for we uncovered in one day as many as one hundred and forty-six inscribed stones.

The excavations did not proceed without difficulties. We had quite a problem in making a satisfactory explanation to the Caid and the natives as to the whys and wherefores of our digging in the most sacred of all Tuareg tombs. Chapuis, our guide, explained to them that the *bordj* was of French origin. "You," he offered in proof, "build your houses of thatch and bamboo, while this is built of stone, and, as you know, all the houses of the white man are built of stone."

This was a bit thin, even for a native, but for the moment they let us proceed in peace, which gave Chapuis time to think up another story to appease them. Upon their second return he tried to explain that Queen Tin Hinan had nothing whatever to do with their history; that she was a lady who lived long before their ancestors came to this land. I am of the opinion that they then knew poor Chapuis to be a man capable of exhibiting every carelessness with the truth, for it is well known throughout the country that Queen Tin Hinan was mother of the Tuareg, and that she was buried here with her gallant nobles.

When the tomb was opened it seemed certain that we would have trouble with the Tuareg, but the ingenious Chapuis explained to the natives that the position of the body was contrary to all the Tuareg customs of burial. Another thing in our favor was the fact that the Tuareg believe that all of the ancient tombs of the Hoggar contain the bones of Djinns, great giants or spirits, and they were evidently surprised at the small dimensions of the remains of the Queen.

But I run ahead of my story. It will be better to acquaint the reader with the surroundings and attempt to put him in the proper atmosphere before actually bringing forth the earthly remains of Queen Tin Hinan.

The view from the summit of the ruined edifice is grand indeed. Doubtless, the builders chose the site for its commanding position. In the purple distance can be seen the great Koudia of the Hoggar, with the massive Tahat and the needle-like summit of Mt. Illiman piercing the vivid blue sky. The Koudia has aptly been named by the Tuareg, "The Roof of the Sahara." Like the distant Atlas, these mountains are supposed to uphold the sky, and perhaps this is a reflection of the ancient Greek legend regarding the Atlas Mountains. The Koudia, a range of considerable importance, is the supposed abode of the King of the Djinns, (evil spirits) and few indeed are the natives courageous enough to climb these peaks or visit the surrounding canyons.

The river that passes, in flood time, comes from this range. There are now green trees in the dried-up river bed, and several times our workmen pointed out in the distance flocks of beautiful gazelles, eating the plant life that grows on the banks of the river.

In the midst of our work on the fourth day of excavation, clouds began to cover the distant peaks. They came up suddenly. In a few minutes raindrops began to fall, drops that appeared as large as a silver half dollar. An immense rainbow arched the sky and the workmen told us that it was a sign of a wedding among the spirits of the mountains. As soon as the rain began falling we made a rush for our camp near the river bed, fearing that it might be suddenly swept away by one of those rare and terrible Saharan floods. Such an event is not uncommon in the Hoggar.

In 1904 a cloudburst in that region destroyed many human lives. Our guide, Chapuis, has been marooned on an island for eight days and has floated down a flooded river on a hastily made raft. These adventures took place in the heart of the Sahara, and less than fifty miles from the barren Tanezrouft, the land of thirst, where there is never a drop of rainfall, year in and year out. Only a few people know that in this region are to be found mountains, rivers, waterfalls and green valleys of trees. This territory, not quite as large as Switzerland, is surrounded on all sides by hundreds of miles of dreadful desert land.

The approaching storm alarmed us considerably. We feared it would destroy our caravan of supplies, which we knew was following the river bed as the best route to our camp. Rations were low, and if the food did not arrive within a few hours, we might be faced with the prospect of making an effort to cook some of the vegetable matter found in the temple storeroom, and which had lain there for perhaps two thousand years.

When the first drops of rain began to fall our negro workmen magically disappeared. They cannot stand the touch of water, and it was ludicrous to see them hide their heads in different corners of the excavation, leaving their bodies exposed to the downpour.

As soon as the rainfall had ceased, we continued removing the pile of rock, in an effort to gain entrance to the central room, where legend and history placed the sepulcher of the Queen. As we were digging there it came to our minds that perchance Pierre Benoit, the famous novelist, might have been familiar with some of the legends concerning Queen Tin Hinan, and these legends furnished him with the inspiration to write his famous "Atlantide." In this rather striking novel, Benoit tells the story of a mysterious woman who lived in the Hoggar, was a descendant of the "Atlantis," and was known as Neptune's daughter. He says that this was the last remaining colony of the Lost Continent – the sole survivors of that calamitous spasm of Mother Earth which took place some nine thousand years before Christ.

Benoit says that in the rocky fastness of the Hoggar dwelt Antinea, whose lovers were the lost explorers of the Sahara. They were entrapped or betrayed into her hands by her faithful Targui, Sheik Ben Chehr (one of Colonel Flatters' assassins), who carried the victims to her wonderful palace in the Hoggar. After a time they died of love, and were mummified and placed in a central room with the dates of their birth and death on each casket. Such was the fancy and fiction of Benoit. Surprising as it may seem, the massive tomb into which we were then digging is the last resting place of a great Queen, and around the base are twelve sepulchers of twelve nobles. What a strange coincidence that a fictionist should so nearly approach fact!

On the sixth day of our work our food supplies were completely exhausted and a Tuareg guide departed for Tamanrasset, in search of our delayed or lost caravan. Chapuis and I continued removing tons of rock and sieving countless trays of sand.

On the seventh day we reached a storeroom in the center of the monument. Leading to the room was a small stone doorway covered with inscriptions, and it is here that great events were soon to take place. Our excitement was intense. After four days spent in cleaning out the room, we came to a large leather covering which bore beautiful fringes and strange designs – the first thing of its kind that has ever been found in the Sahara. It soon became apparent that this covering was stretched from one side of the room to the other and this unusual drapery gave us the feeling that we were on the point of making a great discovery.

While removing the accumulated dirt and sand of centuries from this wonderful piece of ancient workmanship, I found a cornelian bead. A cry of joy escaped, for here in my hand was a link with the ancient past! The object was identical with the cornelian beads found in the excavation of the Temple of Tanit, at Carthage, and it caused me to wonder if we were on the track of a Carthaginian culture that in ages past had found its way into the heart of the desert.

After we had carefully removed the leather covering, we found a huge burial stone, and so great was our excitement over this new find that we could hardly wait to clear the room so that we might lift this stone which covered the entrance to an underground room. For hours we worked unceasingly on the rocks piled on the central stone. So great was our industry that the dust and dirt nearly choked us.

We had the feeling that the Royal Chamber was underneath, and we worked with the enthusiasm of hounds on a trail. Chapuis was nearly as enthusiastic as I, but not quite, for he had been disappointed so many times in the opening of tombs, to discover, after all the labor, that the body had been eaten by ants or carried away. He kept saying again and again, "I do hope the ants have not eaten it away."

One of the strange phenomena of the Saharan tombs is the disappearance of the bodies caused by the onslaught of a flying ant, known as the termite. These pests find their way into ancient sepulchers and devour all the bones, as well as all objects less durable than stone itself. "Sometimes only the teeth are left behind," Chapuis said sadly, "for the termites are thoughtless destroyers. I feel they have been here, too."

We toiled on, hour after hour, from sunset to sunrise, occasionally coming out of the burial chamber for a breath of air and to have a look at the towering peaks in the distance and also in the hope of catching sight of our food caravan. The pestilent flies, the heat, the dust, and the dreadful odor of the Tuareg negro slaves, all served to make it a labor that would have been intolerable but for the feverish zeal incident to our find. I distinctly recall how my hopes fell at one time, when Chapuis lost courage and proclaimed that there was no use going on. He declared that the tomb was surely bare. In support of his contention he pointed to traces of the dreadful flying ants. But I remembered past experiences in the excavation of Utica and Carthage, and prevailed upon Chapuis to dig deeper, telling him that many of the tombs at Carthage were found at a depth of over ninety feet.

As the digging went on we were surprised to find ourselves in a room hewn out of solid rock. What a monotonous work it must have been with the primitive instruments of those days. It was early in the morning of October 18, 1927, that Chapuis and I, alone in the tomb, uncovered a crystal vase – the forerunner of a series of discoveries which startled the scientific world.

Several times during the work, the natives were on the point of abandoning us, partly due to the difficulty of the work and also because of their superstitions – though I am confident that a native can create superstition if he thinks it will assist him in escaping labor. They had already declared that the great storm, as it passed over, was the wrath of the gods directed upon us for disturbing the tomb. When by ill fortune we found several snakes, and especially large scorpions, the natives promptly vowed that this was a direct warning from the evil spirits and that we must at once desist from desecrating the sacred tomb.

Our greatest worry, however, was the food question. Our store of supplies was exhausted, even to the hated beans that had kept us going for nearly a week. It is taxing to carry on the arduous labors connected with excavation when such work must be done on an empty stomach, though it is remarkable how little one thinks of bodily comforts when treasure hunting of this sort begins to show results. I now recall that, when working in the tomb, no thought was given to the food question.

Under the ancient leather covering was a room filled with treasure sufficient to keep us excited for several days. When the remains of the Queen were discovered, our joy was supreme, but our first job was to keep the Tuareg and natives from knowing the extent of our discovery. To this end we kept a strict guard at the entrance of the tomb. We dared not let them see the amazing treasure of the rock chamber. In Africa, the mere mention of gold is enough to lay yourself open to all sorts of risks.

Queen Tin Hinan was wrapped in painted leather with traces of gold leaf. Among the bones were found that beautiful collection of jewels that are to-day the chief treasure of the Bardo Museum in Algiers. The laborious and slow work of sieving now took a large part of our time, for nearly all the earth in the funeral chamber contained beautifully worked golden beads, emeralds, cornelians, and amethysts. All this richly rewarded our efforts, but what with the heat, the flies, the wind and hunger, our task was not easy.

By this time the natives had guessed that something important was going on and sensed that the tomb was revealing rich secrets. Our strict guard confirmed them in this supposition. Chapuis overheard the negro foreman of the natives say that the strangers had found gold, much gold, and that he was a stupid man indeed not to have guessed about the hidden treasure and dug it up himself long ago.

At one time, while removing a gold bracelet from the arm of the Queen, I looked up and was startled at seeing several pairs of dark eyes watching us through the doorway above. "Tuareg nobles," I whispered to Chapuis.

"It is a very bad sign," he replied. "Doubtless they have been told by the negro foreman that we are making astounding discoveries and the rascal has exaggerated it a hundred times."

Several times I climbed out of the tomb with the feeling that eyes were watching us, but by the time I had climbed out of the rock chamber, I could never discover where the veiled visitors had vanished. It was a weird feeling, this being continually watched by unseen eyes.

As time went on we became more firmly convinced that the Tuareg from the mountains had been advised of what was taking place, and were secretly gathering in the neighborhood of the tomb. For that reason we began earnestly to pray that the relief party would soon reach us. We were only four. A surprise attack could easily be planned and executed, as our camp was surrounded by tall Soudan grass and thick bamboo trees.

Although we never saw anyone, save on that one occasion when I saw them looking into the tomb, we felt that they were all around us, and this feeling was considerably heightened by our knowledge of the Tuareg. He comes and goes like a wraith of the desert; he is as familiar with the secrets of keeping well hidden as any wild creature of this earth.

At night we heard sounds, somewhat disturbing, that seemed to indicate that the Tuareg were surrounding and approaching nearer to the camp. We kept our revolvers handy and one of us always stood guard. Later we learned from the lips of the French officers at In Salah that a Djich was after us, composed of several hundred guns! We learned that this small army of raiders had formed in the mountains of Morocco and had passed within sixty miles of our encampment. This may seem a wide margin of safety, but transport yourself to the Sahara and become a member of a party of four against several hundred Tuareg, and you will feel that the margin is none too wide. Had they found us we would have utilized the tomb as a fortress until relief came – if it arrived in time.

The attack of the Tuareg is always swift and sudden. The speed they make, both in their approach and in their escape, is beyond comprehension. They are mounted on the famous giant Mehari camel, beautiful beasts capable of extraordinary speed. A raiding party of Tuareg may be seen in the Matmata Mountains, and in a few days be a thousand miles away, disappearing with their booty into the far and inaccessible reaches of the Djouf or the Rio Del Oro.

Although we were quite anxious concerning the possibility of an attack, the food question had become so serious that we were at last forced to procure from the natives some of their horrible messes. Their chief dish is a mixture of grain and honey, with bits of snakes and bugs. To add to its flavor, they sprinkle in a handful of ants. It is considered a great delicacy when the dish is garnished with locusts and grasshoppers. When first faced with this dish we agreed to starve rather than attempt to eat the mess.

We decided, therefore, to give up our work at the tomb until we could secure some food. We left one man on guard while the rest of us went out to try to obtain a gazelle. I was fortunate enough to shoot a young gazelle and the steaks taken from that young and beautiful beast were highly appreciated by the small group of men who for ten days had been on exceedingly short rations, and for the past two days without any food whatsoever. This feast renewed our strength. For a few more days the work in the tomb went on at a great pace. We were careful to remove all the earth from around the Queen's remains, so that we could make good photographs and drawings of the skeleton exactly as it was found.

Near the head of this long-buried queen of the Sahara we collected a considerable group of strange objects. Besides the crystal vase already spoken of, we found a statuette of a prehistoric woman, similar to those found in the prehistoric caves of southern France. This statuette is about nine inches in height, and shows the form of the female body as it was in the early paleolithic times. When we first uncovered that strange little statuette we did not realize that it would become a subject for controversy all over the scientific world.

To this day we do not understand how this prehistoric work of art could have found its way into a tomb built so many thousands of years later. Possibly it was kept in the home of the queen as an idol that had descended from generation to generation since the earliest days of man. Again, is it not reasonable to suppose that Queen Tin Hinan was somewhat interested, in a limited way, in the history of those who had gone before her, and realizing, even in her day, that this was a rare bit of prehistoric sculpturing, prized it for what it was and kept it in her palace? Her interest in it would have served to convince members of her court that it was one of her prized possessions and, following the custom of the day, they buried it with her.

To the right of the queen's skull we found the sculptured bowl that later was to give us the date of the tomb. It was exceedingly difficult to place the epoch of the objects found around the queen. In a discussion over the discovery, at the *Institute de France,* there was a diversity of opinion among the scientists, and the gap separating them from agreement was as great as fifteen centuries!

It was soon apparent to us, as we worked in the tomb, that the queen had worn a diadem of precious stones, and that these had fallen from a leather band that crossed her forehead. We also found the stones of earrings, the mountings of which had disintegrated, leaving only the emeralds.

Around the queen's neck was the extraordinary spectacle of over three hundred precious and semi-precious stones, all of which became beautiful indeed when we washed them and placed them in the brilliant sunshine to dry. But the thing that astonished us most, as our trembling hands uncovered object after object, was the amazing collection of bracelets on the arms of the queen. On the right arm we found nine huge solid gold bracelets, of a weight quite surprising.

On the left arm were eight solid silver bracelets of exactly the same design as those on her right arm. These bracelets were as shining and bright as the day they had been put on the queen for the last time. One night, while working in the tomb at a late hour, we lit up the treasures with our electric torches, and I shall never forget how the whole room fairly glittered with the flashing light of the radiant, brilliant jewels.

We found a complete series of the queen's toilet articles – parts of a bronze mirror, a pair of rusty scissors, a number of knives, and what appeared to be hairpins. There were three ostrich plumes lying across her head, but these, as well as the thin white veil that once must have covered the skull, entirely disappeared as soon as they were touched! Strangely enough, there were no rings on her fingers.

Only after we had uncovered the skeleton did we discover that the body was reposing on a magnificent bed of hand-carved wood, interwoven with colored cloth and leather thongs, all held together by beautifully worked leather tassels. A strange and as yet unexplained detail of this bed was that the carved wood came from a region alien to the Sahara. Many of the jewels and beads found around the body were similar to those found in my excavations of the Temple of Tanit, and were distinctly of Phoenician origin.

As the work continued, more and more objects came to light, increasing our enthusiasm until Chapuis, Martini (no, no! He was the automobile mechanic), Bradley Tyrell, and myself were entirely oblivious to the rest of the world. Our excitement and eager enthusiasm hourly increased as we slowly uncovered the objects around the body, and it is no exaggeration to say that some work of art came out every two or three minutes.

We found one magnificent necklace made of a number of golden stars, to which hung a perfect example of a Greek column in solid gold. Everything that came to light added to our mystification. From whence came these objects? What was that strange civilization that could bury works of art in the heart of the world's greatest wilderness?

It was difficult for us to sleep at night, so great was our eagerness to carry on the work. We would lie on our backs, wrapped in our furs, gazing up at the inverted bowl of a blue heaven studded with its millions of shining stars, and in our minds we would be trying to form some mental picture of the famous legendary queen who had become a reality. Probably she was some Joan of Arc of her day, considered by the ancient people as half witch and half divinity.

To have been buried with such pomp, she must have collected most of the riches of that desolate country as a tribute to past heroic deeds. If not a great leader, then certainly she must have been a great ruler. She may have been both. We later opened the tombs of several of the nobles surrounding the base of the mountain, but none of these tombs were filled with precious stones or other objects of value, although traces of swords and armor were found there.

It is difficult to describe in cold print the scene in the rock sculptured chamber of the queen. The bracelets, the tiaras, the crystal vase, the remains of the magnificent platform on which the venerated ruler had been laid to rest – such things so thrill the heart of the explorer that he finds difficulty in imparting that thrill to the reader. Nor can he adequately describe the expression on the faces of his fellow explorers, in their awe and surprise at finding such an amazing treasure in one of the most God-forsaken spots in the world.

As the scientific points of the discovery were completed such as the measurement, the weighing, the drawing and photographing of the objects we slowly and carefully placed these treasures in specially made boxes. Our moving picture operator was constantly on the job. Not a scene, not a single discovery, was forgotten by him. All of the details of the discoveries were filmed one by one as they appeared.

One of the most vivid scenes of this historic film documentation is a view from one of the opposite hills, showing the excavation of the great sepulcher in full swing. It looks as if a volcano had suddenly sprung into eruption. The negroes are seen throwing the boulders and rocks over the side of the edifice, a cloud of dust is rising in the air, and one can distinctly see the speed and enthusiasm with which the work progressed.

But even as we worked, danger was in the air. On the night that the magnificent gold bracelets were brought to light, we knew that in some fashion the natives and the Tuareg tribesmen had learned of the discovery of much gold.

That night, while sleeping peacefully and soundly, I received one of the most sudden shocks of my desert experience. We had established our camp on a slightly elevated spot, with a palisade of bamboo and bushes to keep off the cold night winds that came out of the mountain. I was fast asleep, and doubtless dreaming of still richer finds, when I was rudely brought back to the hazards of present day life by the roaring discharge of a gun within a few inches of my ear.

The day had been long, the labor exhausting, and my slumbers were profound. The shock of the exploding rifle seemed to sear my brain. It appears that Chapuis, on seeing a figure slowly crawling towards our encampment, had not hesitated to shoot. We were all on our feet in a moment, though I was holding my head in my hands. Martini seized his gun; Bradley Tyrell immediately began firing his revolver into the bushes. We will never know whether we wounded the creeping man, whom Chapuis swore he saw in the moonlight, and he further declared that he saw the gleam of a knife held in the mouth of the night stalker.

After that moment of excitement we renewed the camp fire. There was no more sleep for any of us that night. We sat vigilantly on guard. Time and again, during our vigil, the firelight reflected from the luminous eyes of some beast prowling in the thicket. The following morning we found distinct tracks indicating that some one had been propelling himself toward our camp on hands and knees. My only wonder is that the Tuareg, who were unquestionably hiding in the vicinity, did not spear us as we slept.

Professor Reygasse has told me that once, while sleeping in a desolate region of the Tidikelt, a spear suddenly ripped through his tent and buried itself in the sand within a few inches of his body, and though everything was done to discover whence came this murderous weapon, not even a footprint was found. The Tuareg knows how to cover up his tracks!

The unexplained delay in the arrival of our caravan of supplies was certainly known to the Tuareg and had given them confidence. At one time we thought that we had better move our camp up into the tomb, and would have done so but for the thought that such a move might convince the Tuareg that we realized the danger of our position. It is difficult to describe the sensation of sleeping far away from civilization with the full knowledge that within a few yards of where one is reposing lurks the death that has made Saharan history so dreadful.

But the work went on. One day, while we were busily excavating in the now familiar rock chamber, the sound of a gun and a series of yells and shouts brought us hurriedly to the top of the parapet. What a welcome sight met our eyes! Outlined on the horizon, and approaching camp, was our long looked-for caravan. With our powerful glasses we could distinguish our New York Times correspondent, Harold Denny, followed by jolly Alonzo Pond, who was leading a number of camels. Our first moment of joy was dampened somewhat by the realization that our motor cars were not in the caravan. Something had happened to prevent their arrival and we were robbed of the consolation that we could escape attack through the speed of the Renault cars.

As the caravan approached we left the tomb and ran down the empty river bed to greet our friends. Our physical appearance gave them quite a shock, for we had lost many pounds in weight.[1]

Our first act was to announce, somewhat breathlessly, the great discovery; the second was to inquire how many boxes of conserves they had brought with them. Though we were half famished at the moment, we had enough strength to display some of the treasures before we ravenously attacked a dozen boxes of sardines.

---

1.   Upon my return to civilization I found that while on the expedition I had lost thirty-six pounds.

We were keenly disappointed to learn that the gasoline caravan, which had been sent out three months earlier, had not yet arrived at Tamanrasset, with the result that we were now faced with the prospect of having our party enlarged without the satisfaction of being certain of the time of the arrival of our food and gasoline.

But hope must be the ever-present ally of those who joust with fortune in the desert. There was nothing for us to do but to continue our work and watch the far horizon with hopeful eyes for the appearance of our motor caravan. On the fourth day after the arrival of the correspondent and Alonzo Pond, the motors came thundering into camp. Professor Reygasse and Count de Beaumont, resident governor of the territory, arrived with the caravan. Count de Beaumont was accompanied by some of his Mehari desert guardians – a truly welcome company!

Our first thought was to take our fill of food. After we had eaten ravenously, we joyously presented Professor Reygasse with the magnificent objects taken from the tomb. He was pleased and excited beyond words. Count de Beaumont, as soon as he realized the extent of the discovery, made arrangements to send a special messenger back to the wireless station at Tamanrasset to inform the Governor-General of Algeria of the extent of the discovery and to offer the treasure to the National Museum of Algiers. This was a splendid opportunity for the New York Times correspondent. He was promptly lifted up into his Seventh Heaven. "Think of it!" he shouted. "We have three whole columns for three consecutive days on the front page!"

Think of it, indeed! Three front page displays was his measure of this discovery, while we were thinking that for years to come, scientists, scholars, and all those interested in the all too little known history of a vanished civilization, might come to some suitable museum and there learn more of the upward march of man.

That night we had a great celebration. We made a huge bonfire, fired our guns into the air, and drank a few bottles of good old Bergundy. Alonzo Pond, he of the jolly heart and high spirit, composed the following dedicatory verse in honor of my discovery – although in so doing he drew freely from the doughboys' World War classic:

> Comte de Prorok went over the top
> Parlez vous,
> Comte de Prorok went over the top
> Parlez vous,
> Comte de Prorok went over the top
> And found the grave of a Hottentot,
> Hinky-dinky, parlez vous!

Our next important work was to catalog and pack into the cars the treasures from the tomb. The grand total came to 48 cases. This work went forward rapidly. After cleaning up the whole of the tomb, we put the great stone cover in place and made ready to leave. We also made a good passage way to the central room so that any chance visitors to the region might enter without danger or inconvenience. After a final moving picture scene of the closing of the tomb we rode northward to the canyons to the south of the Hoggar.

Before reaching the fortress of In Salah we had one more narrow escape from certain death. During the night, while camping under the lee of a great rock, I was suddenly awakened by an object falling upon my sleeping bag. I remember giving a sudden jump, and with thoughtless muscular reaction pushed the object off my bed. Unfortunately it fell on the bed of the moving picture operator, who was sleeping next to me. He, in turn, awoke with a most frightful yell, and this was quickly followed by the crack of a gun.

By this time everyone was awake and on his feet, wondering what it was all about. Again it was Chapuis, the "sand dog," as we called him, who alone knew what was going on.

In the bright moonlight we saw him, gun in hand, running off into the distance. In a few seconds we heard another shot, and Chapuis' shout, "I got him!" Barth, the operator, claimed that I had thrown a snake in his face, but when we came up to where Chapuis stood staring at the ground, we found that we had escaped from something far worse than the most venomous snake. A dreaded ouragen,[1] a member of the lizard family, had fallen off the rock on to my bed, and then had been catapulted onto Barth, who claimed that he actually felt one of the claws of the murderous reptile scratch his mouth.

Luckily for both of us, our nervous reaction had been so swift that the ouragen had been thrown off before it could bite. In all the Sahara there is nothing more feared than the bite of this reptile. A frightful and sudden death is sure to follow, for there is no known antidote. Chapuis had dispatched the animal with his shotgun, and so close was the range that we were prevented from preserving the specimen for a museum. The ouragen is about eighteen inches in length, and has four sharp teeth seated in poison sacs. Chapuis told us that in his thirty years of experience in the Sahara, he had seen but one other specimen of this murderous, crawling desert reptile.

On our return journey to In Salah we passed through a Tuareg encampment where our interpreter, Belaid, in return for a few presents, obtained some information regarding a mysterious tomb lying on the unexplored plateau of the Mouydir. We journeyed a score of miles out of our way in the hope of reaching the plateau where these tombs were said to be located, and great was our surprise to come upon a dozen large pyramids located in what appeared to be the crater of an ancient volcano. Here was a find indeed, but we were not prepared to exploit it. We took some pictures, filmed the interesting spectacle with the movie camera, and

---

1.   A lizard-like reptile, so little known that dictionaries are of no help in the search for its proper spelling. The author takes a chance.

regretfully continued our way north. This is but another
proof of what great things are still to be found in this once
thickly populated mountain kingdom.

In the region of Tadjounut we camped in the bed of a
dried-up lake. In antiquity this lake must have been spotted
by pleasant islands, for we found great quantities of prehistoric hatchets and flints. The cars were already so heavily
loaded with the results of our excavations at the tomb, and
the hundreds of Tuareg ethnographical objects and works of
art collected during our stay in the Hoggar, that we could
carry away only a few specimens of the beautifully worked
paleolithic hatchets found on the shores of this dead lake.

Our arrival at In Salah, the French Saharan fortress, was
heralded by a troop of Mehari soldiers, sent out to greet us
and escort us to the walled city in triumphant fashion. The
commander of the fortress, having learned of the successful
results of the expedition, staged a spectacular review in the
courtyard of the citadel, with all the garrison and natives
lined up in a great square.

That night at headquarters we held a party that wanted
nothing in the matter of rejoicing. Every bottle of champagne and wine that could be found was used up in a surprisingly short time. The evening's festivities terminated by the
commander bestowing upon Professor Reygasse and myself
certain Saharan decorations. The officers of the fortress
were so delighted to have as their guests a party of a dozen
more or less young people that at four o'clock in the morning
we were still making merry to the tune of a sand-filled phonograph placed in the central courtyard.

The next morning the Governor ordered a salute of guns
as our motor cars slowly departed from the fortress. A hundred of the magnificent Mehari camel corps were lined up
on either side of the cars and accompanied us for several
miles on our way.

To me it was a dramatic spectacle. Here were these men
of the desert, descendants of an ancient civilization, rever-

ently following their queen on her last voyage. And what a strange voyage for such a queen! The twelve-wheeled Renault, bearing her bones, became a juggernaut, carrying in state a queen who, to her people, had become a deity. And who would dare say it was to be her last voyage? The flight of centuries is sure and certain; "The Sahara is still the Sahara." To-day her remains and all her precious possessions lie in a suitable museum at Algiers, but greater cities than this have been swallowed by the greedy sands, and it is far easier to reconstruct the past than it is to make one single accurate guess concerning the future.

"The Ball no question makes of Ayes and Noes,
But Here or There as strikes the Player goes,
And He that tossed you down into the Field,
He knows about it all – He knows – He knows!"

Chapter 6

SAHARAN IMPRESSIONS

"In solitary length the Desert lies
Where Desolation keeps his empty court,
No bloom of spring, o'er all the thirsty vast
Nor spiry grass is found; but stands instead
In sterile hills, and rough rocks rising gray.
A land of fears! where visionary forms,
Of grisly spectres rise from out the sands. . .

Whatever the mission and objectives of an exploration into the Sahara, and however successful or fruitless may be the result, the explorer, upon his return, faces from the layman the ever present question: "What is the desert like?" "Is it as fearsome and dangerous as pictured?" "Are the Arabs wild and treacherous?"

Some of the fairer questioners will invariably lead up to the question of sheiks, their manners and customs, and the possibility of a lady being carried away into the desert on the back of a spirited Arab stallion. The first three questions are natural and deserve extended reply, especially since we are all world-travelers at heart, even though much of the journeying must be done on the wings of a book while we sit at ease in some sheltered fireside niche. As to the last question, observation prompts the reply that those propounding it have, as a rule, no great reason for alarm. The sheik, after all, is quite a clever fellow, and never blind.

In order to give the reader some impressions of the Sahara, it may be as well to resort to the most graphic method, i.e., the relating of a few personal experiences. This is done with the hope that the reader will pardon the writer for stepping boldly into his book. The experiences will be real rather than fanciful, and will be confined to those which might happen to anyone who tries his luck in the Sahara.

A sand storm is a thing which no desert traveler may hope to long escape, and while it provides one with an experience quite out of the ordinary, few indeed are they who ask for an encore. The sand storm most vivid in my memory struck us upon the desolate, bone-strewn plateau that follows the left bank of the Oed Mia. Our caravan of motors had been halted to make some repairs on one of the Renaults, which we had nicknamed "Lucky Strike." It was a perfect day, with not a hint of breeze, and the sun was beating down mercilessly. There was not a sign to warn us that a sand storm, in all its fury, was to close that peaceful day – at least it had become peaceful following the completion of repairs on "Lucky Strike."

We were lunching quietly in the dunes near Bir Berkane, when suddenly from nowhere came a gust of wind. One look was sufficient. "Quick!" I shouted. "We must get away at once and try to outrun that storm."

To my mind the sand storm is the most horrible experience of all Saharan travel, save, of course, that dreaded horror, thirst. As a rule the storms begin with little or no warning, and there is never enough time for preparation of any kind. Swirling, gray-yellow masses of sand rise from the desert floor, obscuring the horizon like an advancing blanket. The air becomes chokingly oppressive, so hot in fact as to resemble the draft that bites into your face when the doors of an oven are suddenly opened.

We soon had the recalcitrant "Lucky Strike" headed for the trail at top speed, with the wind rising faster and faster and hotter and hotter behind us. Particles of sand – the advance scouts – were already upon us. We at once put on our sand glasses and wrapped around our faces as many veils as possible. Even now our throats were parched and filled with sand. At such a time it is not difficult for one to imagine the possibility and horror of death by suffocation. We recalled how our moving picture operator, G. Barth, when trying to film a sand storm in the Great Erg, had his hands badly cut by the extreme velocity of the sand-filled wind.

It was now getting darker and darker. The sun appeared as it sometimes does in a London fog – yellow, indistinct, and indescribably weird. The landscape seemed to be moving as the storm gained on us, and the whole surface of the earth was advancing in wave-like masses of sand. It was as if the winds were advancing *a la* "Birnam Wood," swirling, eddying and forming little sand ridges such as one sees on the bottom of a troubled shore line.

The sand dunes became enormously exaggerated in the half light, their summits smoking like a series of volcanoes that seemed to wave, to move forward, then back, to this side and to that – the inanimate made animate and drunken by the wine of the winds. The imagination of the Saharan tribes has been played upon by this phenomenon of the sand storm, and to them the whirlwinds of sands are the waltzes of the Djinns – the dancing of the evil spirits.

As we rushed on before the storm our minds ran back to the many desert stories of caravans that had been enveloped and obliterated by the dreaded sand storm. Many of these stories are but the imaginings of the superstitious Oriental brain, but they have some foundation in fact. For example, history tells us how the great army of Cambyses, on its way to pillage the Temple of Jupiter-Ammon at Siwa, was swallowed up entirely by an especially terrific storm.

We raced along, hoping to escape a similar fate. At last the car came to a stop; the trail which had been quite indefinite was now entirely obliterated and we lost sight of the occasional small pillars of stone that mark the trail through the dunes. We must not lose the trail at this time. Chapuis, the sand dog, and myself, stepped from the car in an effort to locate the trail. We advanced cautiously into the inferno of swirling desert, making small signal cairns so as to find our way back. At one moment I lost sight of the car and was unable to find my recently erected markers, but luck was with me and I got back safely. In the meantime, however, Chapuis had wandered off and disappeared into the swirling sand among the dunes.

I was extremely anxious. Our water supply was nearly exhausted, as well as our food, and during the last few miles we had been replenishing a leaky radiator with drinking water. It is strange how, in such a moment, the thoughts go back to cool drinks that have been enjoyed in the past. I have been caught in many skin-searing sand storms, and invariably my thoughts turned to a cold bath and to divers bars and restaurants where are to be found many favorite drinks.

On our expedition to the Hoggar we had with us one gentleman who, at times when a crust of bread and half a can of sardines were to be our ration, would invariably begin talking of some grand meal enjoyed in the past. He seemed thus to put before him a delicious feast, entirely satisfying to himself. He could imagine and did so orally – lunching at Fredrick's, or enjoying a Langouste Thermidor at Prunier. Needless to say, this in no way alleviated the agony and mouth-watering of his listeners – hearers is the better word, for it could hardly be said that anyone really listened. Note: The gentleman came through alive.

Upon the reappearance of Chapuis at our car, we decided to run no further risk in searching for the trail but to make ourselves as comfortable (dreadfully inappropriate word) as possible, hoping that we would not be entirely buried under the advancing seas of sand.

As is often the case in the Sahara, the storm abated somewhat at sunset. After considerable effort to move our car through some newly formed dunes, we gave it up at last, long past midnight, and wrapping ourselves in our blankets in a futile effort to keep out the sand, lay down by the side of the car. Through the magic medium of sleep we were soon wandering along the cool meadow streams of France, of England, and of sweet Elysium.

The Sahara, under the mighty sweep of a sand storm, is the most infernal region on earth. And at all times, it seems, there is the wind. The sand dunes are formed by the wind; countless ages of wind have carved the rocks into forms fantastic; the whole mighty desert is one buffeted, tortured, wind-blasted, devil-haunted, God-forsaken waste. Such are the bitter thoughts and denunciations of the traveler caught in a sand storm. He curses it and returns to it again and again!

To me the wind is one of the great afflictions of the desert. It is impossible to describe the state of one's nerves after several days or weeks of the harassing torture of the invisible fiend that sears the eyeballs, cracks the skin, hinders every motion one takes, and finally reaches into the very brain and makes a hodge-podge of that.

Damn the wind in the Sahara! I hate it more than words can tell. But at night, when the wind dies out, when the sand ceases to scurry, when the sun splashes down and turns the sand clouds into a golden burnished veil, when that inexplicable desert peace envelopes the landscape, then the fighting of the day is forgotten, forgiven, and I love again the mystery of the desert and the inspiring grandeur of the land.

My Worst Day Spent in the Sahara

In the Sahara, never leave camp before the sun rises, and never leave at any time with a broken compass! You can get lost so quickly that you haven't the slightest idea how it happened– in fact, that's why you are lost! You may be only a few miles from camp, possibly only a few hundred yards, but you are lost all the same. At first one is quite angry and chagrined over one's own stupidity; then as time passes anger and chagrin is followed by exhaustion, and on the heels of exhaustion comes fear and then comes madness!

I passed through all of these sensations save the latter one – one day on our way to Ghadames. We had been camping by a little water hole near the great Hamada El Homra, and in the hope of getting game of two kinds – a gazelle and some Libyan inscriptions – I resolved to penetrate into a rocky region and to follow for some distance a dried-out water course. One of our cars had broken down, and it would take three or four hours of the early morning for the mechanics to make the repairs.

Feeling sure that I would have no trouble in the matter of direction, I took my gun, compass and glasses, and pushed off before dawn, intent on exploring a few miles of the region.

As the first glimmer of dawn appeared I found that the terrain was quite uniform and was sprinkled with dark gray sunburned rocks of volcanic formation, interspersed with sand dunes. For two hours I followed the old river bed, examining the rocks for traces of the primitive rock sculptures that are common finds in some of the most desolate parts of the Sahara. But the quest was fruitless, and I had just decided to follow another old river bed when it occurred to me that it would be wise to get my bearings. I climbed to the top of what I thought to be a commanding mass of stone, but upon reaching the summit found that there were innumerable rock hills on either side, all of uniform height and form. Beyond was the far horizon of mountains circling around me, garbed in the pale lavender hues of the early dawn. They, too, took on a confusing uniformity.

However, I made certain conclusions concerning my directions and then decided to return by a fresh trail in order to explore some new territory. Fully convinced that the camp was due west, I turned south and climbed for another hour through the monotonous, never ending hills. By that time the sun was well up in the sky. I began to feel its warming rays. After another half hour I hastened my footsteps and soon found myself almost at a trot, but moving in what I thought was the right direction. The sun was now beginning to beat upon the blackened stones and I was becoming thirsty.

I now began to feel foolish. I was already late and delaying the start, and time was a precious element in our rush across the desert to Ghadames. Then followed anger. The confounded hills were all the same size, color and height. My gun became increasingly heavy, the sun hotter, and my thirst quite tormenting. All around me was a sea of infernal rocks. It seemed that I climbed a score of them in an effort to catch sight of the camp. I kept going west for another hour. The loneliness and silence was becoming appalling. The sky was ablaze. My brain began to whirl. I kept thinking of Barth, the great German explorer, who in the Hoggar of Adjzer had wandered from his camp and became lost while exploring the "Mountain of Spirits." He was only a few miles from his caravan, and his escape from death was nothing short of miraculous.

After thinking of Barth for awhile, I remembered Count de Bruce telling me once of how two of his French soldiers had become lost only a few miles from Ouargla and had perished of thirst and madness.

Distressing thoughts! I fired off my gun, hoping that the others would find me by the sound. No reply. Another hour of tramping. I began to feel hopeless, tired and dull. My clothes were dripping with perspiration. I tried to be calm and to think out how I could help the others find me. If only they would climb to some high point where they could look down on me. I built pyramids of stones on the rocks, to serve as signals to the party who would surely make a line and comb the region, and I began praying that they would find the cairns.

The heat was now intense; I felt as if I were wandering in circles and all the time building cairns (when I could find sufficient stones) and shooting off my gun. Why didn't de Waldeck fire his gun – and the rest of them? Where the devil were they! I felt fear, a sort of panicky, icy feeling round the heart, and suddenly felt very tired.

The horizon of dunes seemed trembling and vague in the distant yellow atmosphere, vibrating with the heat. Once more I climbed a great pile of rock and sand, feeling like a drowning man grasping at a straw. But it was always the same story. As soon as I climbed one sand hill there appeared another ahead of me, identical in size and shape with all the others. The brain reeled with dizziness and weakness.

Dimly I remembered Richardson's description in the second volume of his "Travels in the Great Desert" of his terrible adventure when lost only a quarter of a mile from his camp. He had set off to visit the famous mountain called the "Palace of the Demons," the Ksar Djoumoun, and on the return had missed his encampment and had passed a whole day and night hunting for it. Like Richardson, I began to imagine I saw the camp a dozen times. He writes:

"Although the day was pretty well developed, I was amazed at the deception and phantasm of the desert. Every moment a camel loomed in sight that was no camel, there was also a hideous sameness, the reason, indeed, why I was lost, for there were no distinguishing marks. The mounds followed the rocks, the rocks the mounds, then a little plain, then a little sand, then again the plains, the mounds and the rocks, always the same, an eternal sameness!"

I seemed to be able to remember every line of it! By this time the heat and glare were dreadful. The awful desert lassitude overtook me. The blazing sun, beating down on me, was reflected by the rocks and sands with double force. Dimly I remembered Herodotus telling of the desert people who were called the Atarants, and who were known "for cursing the sun." I cursed the sun that day!

The world around me became a vague yellow haze, for the heat affects all distances, and forms become greatly disproportioned. Small hillocks in the distance are distorted into mountains; elevations that seem near are perhaps five miles away. One suffers from the burning of the soles of the feet, and at times it feels as the inquisition tortures must have felt.

I recalled how a great battle was once fought in the desert, the victory attending those who had the thickest soles. The vanquished could not fight well, due to the burning sands which prevented them from lying down. I have seen the water in the flasks that we carry by our sides actually too hot to be drinkable. One must never be without double sun glasses in the dunes, for blindness comes quickly in the same way as it is caused in the Alps by the glare of the snow.

Happily a daze generally overtakes the unfortunate lost one. The brain seems to melt, and the last remembrance is a dancing line of blue on the horizon looking like the bluest of waters, but in reality only a heat mirage. Ah, then comes the hour when you hate the desert!

But night is falling and, as did Richardson, I revived a little with the sudden coolness of the desert night air. But my thirst was agony. As dusk fell I began to see things – camels, people, the cars, all seemed to loom up before me to dissolve again into nothingness and further bitter disappointment. I remember crying a little and laughing, a hollow, hoarse laugh that was echoed back with a metallic sound from the rocks and sands. The echo was the laugh of the Djinns, mocking my last hour.

However, as the night wore on, the cool air was strengthening me more and more and I began to climb sand dunes again, very tired, terribly thirsty, and the brain half numbed by the thirst and panic. Suddenly my eyes caught a finger of light searching the sky. Was it another dreadful illusion? No, the flashes continued and my heart gave a great beat of joy as I realized that the powerful flashlights of the Citroen cars were being thrown into the sky to indicate the way to me! I was saved, but it was many hours before I reached camp, where the wine and water soon revived me. The rest of the party had spent the whole day anxiously scouring the desert in every direction, but they had not found a single one of the little mounds of stones which I had placed as an indication of my whereabouts.

As long as I live I shall never forget that first drink when I reached camp, and it is absolutely beyond my power to describe my sensations during those delicious hours of making up for lost time.

There are other commonplace hardships which come to all who go into the Sahara. I find it very difficult to sleep in the midday heat of the desert, and God help one in a district where flies and mosquitoes abound. The flies are a mighty curse in the Sahara, and with the wind, the heat, and thirst, they make a dreadful combination of human ills. I shall never forget the excavating of a prehistoric tomb southeast of Tamanrasset. The flies must have followed us from the fortress, and I know that several hundred thousands had accompanied our black workmen from the village. They were in our eyes at every moment; they crawled up our noses, into our mouths, and buzzed incessantly in our ears.

I have put my hand out on a table at Touggourt and had it covered with flies in a few seconds, and in the Hoggar, while trying to photograph or take notes, or when excavating the tomb, the curse of the flies was too exasperating for polite words. We finally resorted to having black veils placed over the helmet. This made one hotter but kept the flies off the face. We used to put our sieves over the food to protect it. I shall never forget passing our camp one day – at Abelessa –

on the way to the tomb and seeing our luncheon, which consisted of a hind quarter of a gazelle that we had shot, hanging in a tree. The meat was absolutely black with flies. I ate the gazelle with only a passing thought and wondered if the flies got their fill. Several times photographs have been spoiled by a fly walking on the lens and appearing in the picture as a vague monster. There were millions of flies around Abelessa in the daytime, yet at sunset the atrocious pests completely and mysteriously disappeared. I spent one evening with Bradley Tyrell trying to locate the resting place of the hoard, and though we searched the bushes and trees, and even the sand, we could not locate them. Shaving in the morning becomes a trying experience, when dozens of flies get mixed up with the lather.

There is one great blessing with regard to the heat in the Sahara: it is a dry heat and, therefore, not half so oppressive and weakening as the humidity of New York or the sultry Paris heat. It is so hot sometimes that it seems actually burning, yet I have still been able to make some kind of an effort which would have been entirely impossible in the humid heat at the same altitude of the thermometer. Seventy degrees Centigrade[1] has been observed in the sand dunes, and in June, in the Great Erg, I have felt that my brain was sizzling. It is strange that after freezing all night one goes through the heat of hell the next day, a hell that begins a few hours after sunrise. The extremes in the desert are surprising. We once observed in the Great Erg that a vase of water, half-buried in the sand, was found to be a frozen block next morning.

Of course, the intense heat induces thirst, but I have found one is less thirsty if one drinks less, and I have been able to train myself to a glass of water at midday and another in the evening. Of all the dreaded ills of the Sahara, first and last, it is always the fear of death by thirst that haunts one

---

1.   Gautier, E. F., *Le Sahara.*

and all. It is a land of fear – fear of being lost, of thirst, of massacre, of raids, of sudden illness, and last but not least, the fear that you may fail to accomplish the objectives of your expedition. And when all is done, the hardships borne, the journey ended, the reward certain and civilization and its security once more a part of life then to me comes the fear that my next expedition may be delayed and some secret of the Sahara forever lost.

Chapter 7

DEAD CITIES OF THE SAHARA

"As though the dead cities of the ancient time
Were builded again in the lights of Heaven,
With spires of amber and golden domes,
Wide streets of topaz and amethyst ways."

One of the interesting problems of Saharan exploration
that has held my attention for a number of years is the trac-
ing of old trade routes and caravan trails in the Sahara.[1] We
know from the ancient historians that the Carthaginians used
to hunt with their elephants in the wild Matmata Mountains
and in the forests of South Algeria. We know there was a
continual trade in precious stones from the interior of the
Sahara and the Sudan to the markets at Carthage, Rome, and
the great cities of the Nile.

Since earliest antiquity Africa has been a great slave pro-
ducing continent, and in ancient chronicles we read of expeditions of armed bands into what was then called Libya, in
search of victims among the Garamantians, Nasamones, and
Getulian tribes. We know, too, that there were great cities in
the Sahara that have long since disappeared. The question of
the means of communication and trade routes between these
ancient civilized centers and the outside world is one that
recommends itself to that student with a flare for

---

1.   Prorok, *Ancient Trade Routes from Carthage into the Sahara*, American Geographic Journal, 1925.

"The glory that was Greece
And the grandeur that was Rome."

We have located traces of the old Roman roads far out in the desert, and the general indication of the trade route is to be found in the long line of tombs that lie along obliterated trails that must have been as difficult in antiquity as they are to-day. We know that even the redoubtable Alexander the Great became completely lost with his huge escort while on his way from the seacoast to the Temple of Jupiter-Ammon.

One of the least known sections of the earth's surface is that part of the Sahara known as the Libyan Desert, and certainly it is the most desolate. But strangely enough, in the heart of these great wastes there lived an ancient people who developed a mighty civilization. The oases that made life possible and tolerable for them, are today covered with beautiful and unexplored ruins of lost peoples. The story of those peoples is hidden by the veil of time; their ruins antedate history; their golden temples and palaces are half buried in the desert sands.

It was in the summer of 1926 that we organized an expedition to explore these forgotten cities in the Libyan Oasis of The Faiyum. The expedition was organized under the auspices of the University of Michigan, but the funds for the work were collected from various collaborators.

We made our headquarters at the old Greek city of Karanis, and from the mud bricks of the ancient city we constructed quite a solid camp. The party was made up of a dozen experts in the different branches of archaeological and geographical research.

The first work to be done, before settling down for a long period of excavation, is the proper handling of stores and equipment. Most of the supplies are ordered in London many months before the actual work begins. Then each department of the archaeological research must be attended to so that when the actual discovery begins the photographers, surveyors, members of the drawing department and the commissariat may all go on in a methodical, uninterrupted way.

Imagine, if you will, the plans for the uncovering of a city that once possessed a population of a hundred thousand. There must be a far-seeing plan, method, discipline, and no small amount of patience. This latter virtue is one of the most difficult to acquire, and this is particularly true of the explorer, whose eagerness and enthusiasm are always threatening to run ahead of his preparations.

The actual view of the city, when we first saw it, had the appearance of a vast mound rising rather abruptly from the desert floor. The first thing to be done was to lay the tracks for the trucks which were to bear away the thousands upon thousands of tons of sand and debris.

It was a month before we began digging down from the top of the great mound, but as soon as the sand began to be hauled away the skeletons of the dead city began to take form. Work progressed. The tale of toil would be of no interest to the reader, though it must be borne in mind that exploration in Africa is not alone a matter of finding – there is also the matter of digging, digging, digging! There are clouds of dust and clouds of flies with which to contend, to say nothing of the need for eternal watchfulness.

At last we dig our way into several of the buildings and discover that we are in the midst of a town that had been suddenly abandoned centuries ago. The inhabitants had left everything in its usual place. It seemed that some giant hand had reached down, picked up the entire population and spirited them away. For example, we would remove the sand from a house, find the entrance, with the door still on its hinges, walk through a corridor with wall paintings on either side, enter the bedroom and find the chairs, tables and the bed with its covering, as well as ancient glass and other objects of general daily use, all lying about as though they had been put there the day before.

Our minds grappled with the thought that these objects had been left undisturbed through twenty centuries. Sand is the best preservative of antiquity, and it is generally blessed by all archaeologists. It not only preserves the objects, but it is clean. In North Africa, nearer the sea, the excavations do not bear nearly so rich a treasure as those in the dry region of the Libyan Desert.

As we progressed with the work we found the ancient papyrus writings of the inhabitants of the dead city, and from these writings were able to reconstruct the life of the city almost as completely as we might had it been written down in a great book. From these writings we learned the names of the governors, the sub-governors, the tax collectors, the year in which they lived, the list of houses visited by the tax collectors, and the local events that took place in the town. Descriptions and stories of wars, of raids from the neighboring desert tribes, of months of famine, uncomplimentary things said of unpopular governors, and bold reports of political uprisings and religious controversies – such is the vivid tale of these long buried records.

It is difficult to describe the sensation that comes to one while slowly digging out of the sand an ancient scroll that may give some new information concerning how these people lived, rejoiced, sorrowed, and passed on in the ages long gone by.

One day we had the joy of discovering the house of the local scribe. We found his study. In this room was his library of papyrus, his desk, inkwell, pens, and even his wastebasket. And joy of joys! Over in another room we found a hundred or more discarded manuscripts which this scribe had thrown all in a heap, with never a thought that in some distant day people would come from foreign lands to dig up and cherish the precious documents which he had thrown away as useless.

With the hope that this work may prove of some value to future explorers, as well as of interest to the casual reader, it may be well to briefly outline our somewhat complicated methods of excavating, particularly with reference to the placing of the army of Arab workmen. Each Arab who had had previous experience in such work was placed over six other Arabs, whose duty it was to carry away the sand. With this crew, the leader slowly advanced, carefully dislodging the sand with his pickax. Whenever an object of interest was found this leader's name was taken down so that he might be rewarded at the end of the week.

The rivalry was quite keen, and when we were passing an especially rich section these additional rewards ("baksheesh" it is called) sometimes came to as much as two hundred dollars per day. On one occasion a lucky Arab found a bag of gold in his line of excavation and the reward derived from a percentage of the weight of the gold was quite enough for him to stop work immediately, buy a bit of land in the oasis, and for the remainder of his life treat all work with the scorn it so richly deserves.

One of the most difficult things in excavating is to keep your eyes on the fingers of the Arab workmen. His trained eyes can see a coin, a bead, or a precious jewel far quicker than can the ordinary individual. I recall how at Carthage we once had a young Arab who was a sort of pet, or mascot, of the expedition. One day, as he was passing out of the works to get his weekly pay and go home, I chanced to notice that his cheeks seemed quite as stuffed as the jowls of a provident chipmunk.

It was quite evident that he was either hiding something or was scourged by a tremendous toothache. Two of us jumped on him at once, turned him upside down and shook him until the objects concealed in his mouth came pouring forth upon the ground. It may sound like exaggeration, but there was hardly a spot on that practiced antique expert that did not conceal coins, bits of mosaic, bronze rings, hairpins, ivory buttons, et cetera. It was such an amusing scene that we forgave the young scoundrel on condition that we be allowed to re-enact the proceedings before the moving picture camera. He had some six pounds of antiquities concealed on his body – quite a haul for one day!

In this connection I may add that I often go to the local antique dealers in Tunis and Algiers to buy back objects stolen from our own excavations.

Pay day at Karanis provided us with interesting scenes when hundreds of native children, in their vivid rags, would sit in long lines within the spaces marking the respective villages. As each name was called the boy or girl would come up to the table to receive pay and then run off to their distant villages, some of which were miles away.

It takes hundreds of laborers to remove the sand from a buried city, but however slow and tedious the work, it is an exciting labor when the skeleton outlines of a city begin to appear and the formless begins to take form in streets, houses, public squares, temples, baths, storehouses and palaces.

At the various excavation sites, such as Carthage, Utica, Bulla-Regia and Karanis, we followed about the same line of procedure. We mapped all the new ruins, photographed, in situ, all the objects discovered, and accurately surveyed the entire find so that we could reconstruct the city, if need be.

The work at Karanis was particularly entrancing, for the reason, perhaps, that we knew less about it than some of the other ruins named. In the evening the finds of the day would be brought into camp to be catalogued and packed away for the museums. Day after day dozens of objects would be brought down from the mound, all of them astonishingly well preserved, considering their great age.

There were objects made of glass, their beautiful colors still vivid after so many centuries; richly painted boxes for keeping the family ornaments and toilet articles; hundreds of coins (to be scientifically cleaned in the laboratory); cloths still retaining their brilliant hues; innumerable beads, bits of jewelry, scraps of papyrus, and thousands of pottery forms of various types and uses. Frequently we found ourselves unable to solve the ancient uses of many of the objects, and many an interesting hour was spent around the dining room table, discussing the various objects, and forming our views. How we enjoyed the visits of Mr. Bell of the British Museum, and of Professor Schmidt, the famous German papyrus expert, who could read the ancient documents almost as easily as he would a daily newspaper!

I recall how thrilled and entertained we were by the finding of two letters written by a soldier lad fighting with the distant Roman legions. The letters were to his mother, who lived in this oasis town, and were exactly like the millions of home letters that have always been written by men away at the wars. The boy spoke of his trip to Rome, of his travels and adventures and impressions, and ended by begging his mother not to worry about him for he was visiting beautiful places. He sent his love to all his brothers, sisters and friends. A living, human document from out the dim past.

How little we have changed. The basic human emotions remain about the same. All those lost peoples, into whose histories we were delving with pickaxes and shovels, seem somehow to belong to us through ties of emotional kinship. Ah, they are friends and neighbors, separated only by a score of centuries, which is but an hour in the incomprehensible limits of time!

On another day we made a most exciting discovery. A bag of gold coins came out of the sand, but how it got there, or why, we shall never know. Perhaps it had been dropped when some sudden, calamitous disaster overtook the city. Someone, seeking escape, had held on to his precious gold until he realized that life itself was to be gained or lost, and then quickly abandoned what a moment before had seemed so dear in his eyes. When we came upon these coins they

were shining and glistening among the silver sands, triumphant still in their appeal, despite the fact that for centuries
they had lain smothered in the worthless dross of the desert.
This find recalled to our minds how at Carthage, in the
vicinity of the Temple of Tanit, we found three large vases
filled with hoarded gold coins of the Byzantine period – a
wondrous spectacle when poured out before one.

The desert around the ruins of Karanis is rich in archaeological remains, both historic and prehistoric. There are
ancient cemeteries, nameless temples, and prehistoric sites
reaching far into the desert. For many months, with one or
two companions from the camp, I explored the region west
of the oasis, locating ancient sites, dolmens, strange rock
tombs, and the fossilized bones of many nonexistent animals.

The Oasis of the Faiyum has at least a dozen dead cities,
still to be scientifically excavated, and it is to be hoped that
in the near future the ruins further out in the Libyan Desert
will appeal to some institution which will take over the
costly and patient toil of reclaiming from the desert sands
these treasure cities of a colorful and romantic past.

We discovered an astounding number of beautifully
worked neolithic flints in the desert around Lake Karun.
Thousands upon thousands of arrowheads, spear points and
other human artifacts littered the desert surface all along the
shores of the now rapidly disappearing Lake Moeris. Our
distinguished collaborator, Professor Bovier-Lapierre, who
later communicated the discovery to the Egyptian Institute,
was amazed at the richness of the sites located during the six
months of exploration, and especially those in the little
explored region southwest of the Djebel Katrani.

While exploring the terraces of the high desert that looks
down on Lake Karun, I had the fortune to discover the first
abri sous roch to be found in Egypt. Hundreds of strange,
crescent-shaped flints were found in the cave, and the slopes
below were strewn with unusual implements to which Pro-

fessor Bovier-Lapierre gave the name of "Karunien." Scores of these implements, hatchets and chipped flints, were found embedded in a mass of bone. This discovery was announced in the press, with the consequent result that many adventurers, sightseers and tourists organized unorganized expeditions to push out from Cairo in an effort to locate the site. When I returned a year later, the heretofore trackless desert between Cairo and this site was covered with motor tracks and countless sardine tins!

It is astonishing how many tourist parties will venture into the desert without the proper guides and with little or no preparation. Time after time, during our work, we would have to go out into the desert to search for parties who had left Cairo, a hundred miles away, and were trying to make their way to our excavations. One party of American ladies who had heard of our work immediately set sail in their automobile without taking any of the many necessary precautions. Of course, they were promptly lost and remained so for three days. Their car had broken down. Car after car was sent out to locate them, and these, in their turn, became lost among the sand dunes. Quite a desert hubbub was kicked up by these fearless ladies. We spent our nights building flares on the top of the excavation mounds in an effort to help the lost and foolhardy tourists who were wandering around the desert.

It is surprising how easily one can get lost in a region so monotonous and unchanging in its physical aspects. Recently a party succeeded in getting lost within a few miles of the pyramids, and when found were nearly mad, fighting each other in a lonely cave. On several occasions the Egyptian Government has been forced to use airplanes to locate lost parties, and at last found it necessary to pass a law forbidding anyone to venture into the desert without experienced guides.

The necessity for such a law is proof of the statement that the desert has so strong a call upon the imagination as to blind the thoughtless to its dangers. This is not difficult to understand when one considers that from the banks of the Nile to the Atlantic seacoast, a distance of more than three thousand miles, there lie beneath the sands many cities still to be discovered and uncovered. In the Libyan Desert there are the Oases of Dankla, Farafara and Siwa, all containing beautiful ruins of which very little is known.

We know that somewhere in this region there are still to be found the famous Oasis Zenzura, the "Oasis of the Blacks," the legendary "City of Brass," and the mysterious "City of Copper," mentioned by many of the ancient historians. Further west we have the old caravan trail that leads from Thebes to Carthage, on which we find the old name of Augiles, "The Black Mountain," at a place called Sokna. From there the old trail once led to Ghadames, whose ancient name is so easily recognized in the word Cydamus. To-day this land is called the Fezzan, a name that has come down from the ancient name of Phazanie.

This is the land of the once mighty kingdom of the Garamantians, a people who at one time employed oxen to draw their chariots across the desert. It was Barth who first discovered at Telizzahren the rock sculptures that gave us an indication of how those ancients traveled before the advent of the camel.

At the ruins of Djerma, inscriptions have been found in a language yet unknown, and we have in this region a great field for future archaeological work.

Along the seacoast are the remains of many dead cities, colonies of the Greeks, Phoenicians and Romans. The ruins of Leptis Magna have recently been uncovered by the Italian Government. In the land of the Troglodytes and Nasamones, I have seen many traces of ancient settlements, sometimes only a column here and there above the sand, and at times temples whose beautifully colored walls have been toned into softer shades by the processes of erosion.

On the island of Djerba we visited the ruins of seven distinct cities of which we have practically no history. Doubtless Djerba is the famous island of the "Lotus Eaters,"
mentioned by Homer, and is near the sea-engulfed city of
Tipasa, which we explored several years ago by making use
of Greek divers.[1]

From Morocco, through Algeria and Tunisia, there is one
continual chain of these ancient cities, many of them built of
the beautiful golden-colored Numidian marble. These latter
cities provide a breath-taking spectacle at sunset, when the
vivid North African sunset lights up the columns of the temples with fingers of fire.

At Sbeitla there is a group of temples standing in the
midst of a desolate desert country. A little to the north of this
we find the great amphitheatre El Djem, one of the wonders
of North African architecture. Far up in the now desolate
and savage Numidian Mountains we have what is known as
the Pompeii of North Africa, Bulla Regia (City of the Royal
Baal), the ancient capital of Numidia.

In the heights of the Atlas Mountains we find the ruins of
the ancient city of Khamissa, practically unknown to the visitors of Africa to-day. It is a wonderful relic of the past, situated on the heights above great gorges that contain a series
of large basins, in which are reflected the majestic ruins.
Between the Mountains of the Air and the Hoggar, lies the
lost city of Tafassaset, which we hope to discover and excavate on our coming expedition. Southwest of the Hoggar is
the abandoned city of the Tuareg, called Essouk, once the
capital of a mighty empire but to-day half buried beneath the
ever encroaching sands.

Toward Timbuktu there are many old cities of the negro
and Tuareg empires, still to be excavated and explored. In
antiquity there was a great lake near the present ruins of
Taodeni, the water of which came from the Fauta-Djallon in

---

1. De Prorok, *Digging for Lost African Gods,* The Narrative Press, 2000.

the Atlas Mountains. These waterways became choked by sand and in time the great lake dried up, driving the population away and leaving the land open to the conquering Berber-Tuareg of the north.

The known list of ruins yet to be explored in the Sahara is indeed long – endless tombs and mausoleums in the Hoggar, in the Air at Tibesti, while further south toward the Niger are the desert cities of past empires such as Timbuktu, Gao and Djenne. These regions are filled with legends and strange tales of such mighty rulers as Aski the Great, last of the Songay rulers, and of King Yunus and his bride Isabel. The Christian monarchs ruled here in the Fourteenth Century and had for their capital the lost city of Assode.

The kingdom of Aski, whose capital was Gao, ruled the whole of the Sahara, according to the history of Leo, the African, and that ruler's treasure is supposed to lie buried in a city somewhere south of the Hoggar. The tide of successive empires swept back and forth across the Sahara, and continues to this very day.

For years it has been a part of my objective to find traces of the different empires in Africa, and more particularly that part known as the Sahara. I feel confident that the Egyptians, Carthaginians and Romans have left many traces still to be uncovered. Duveyrier found an Egyptian inscription at Ghadames. Barth found a Getulian and Garamantian drawing at Rhat, known to the Romans as Oppidum Rapsas. I, myself, saw traces of the cult of Jupiter-Ammon on the shores of Djered, and we found Carthaginian beads and Roman coins in the Hoggar.

On the border of Lake Tagi, which lies on the edge of the Sahara, there are found great Bethel stones, recalling the Phallic cult of Carthage and Pompeii. The Songhays claim that they traded with Rome in antiquity, and many of the Peuhl people have survivals of customs that originated in the empires of Egypt and Carthage. The Niger, that great river bordering the Sahara on the south for nearly three thousand miles, has been known since earliest antiquity. Unquestionably it has changed its course, at some date yet undetermined, but its old bed is still to be seen southwest of the Hoggar. This radical change, however slow in its process, would have a marked effect upon the climate, and this may account for the fact that we now find only the ruins of cities where once dwelt a numerous population.

To the west of the Sahara is the land of Mauretania, where in Roman times lived a Berber people called "White Ethiopians." Our next expedition is to take us through the Rio Del Oro and Mauretania, through the little known land south of Morocco on the Atlantic seaboard. If the mystery of the "Lost Atlantis" is to be solved, perhaps it is there. Strangely enough, this region, the most interesting for Saharan studies, is the least known of all.

To-day the fierce Moors rule these unknown and uncharted spaces of desert, oases and mountains. They came here, probably, in the Ninth Century and have held sway ever since. They have a cruel, eagle-like look on their pure Semitic faces, and their ferocious natures and ceaseless raidings have prevented the land from being explored. I feel that the same people who built the Alcazars and Alhambras of Spain may have many hidden and beautiful ruins in the unknown mountains of Mauretania, Rio Del Oro, Lusitania, and southern Morocco.

It will be difficult and hazardous to penetrate this region, but the spell of the unknown interior has a lure too strong to resist. That the way is forbidden makes it doubly appealing and enchanting. The search for knowledge concerning some unknown kingdom is what carries the explorer on through hardships and dangers, heedless of comfort, and willing to accept the hazard.

Fortunately, this lure has been constant since the beginning of history, and a long line of historians have contributed to our knowledge and have served as guides. Many of those historians gave to us what was later called legend, but which in time was proven to be very near the fact.

In Flaubert's "Salambo" we read of the strange peoples of the Sahara: "Nomads from the table-lands of Barca, bandits from Cape Pluscus and the promontory of Dernah, from Phazzana and Marmarica – they crossed the desert, drinking at the brackish wells walled in with camels' bones. The Zuacces, with their covering of ostrich feathers, had come on quadrigae; the Garamantians, masked with black veils, rode behind on their painted mares; others were mounted on asses, onagers, zebras, and buffalos; while some dragged after them the roofs of their sloop-shaped huts, together with their families and idols. There were Ammonians, with limbs wrinkled by the hot waters of the springs; Ataranians, who curse the sun; Troglodytes, who bury their dead with laughter beneath branches of trees; and the hideous Auseans, who eat grasshoppers; the Achyrmachiclae, who eat lice; and the vermillion-painted Gysantians, who eat apes."

Times have not changed since these people existed. Many of their traits have come down to us. The Ammonians still bathe in the Fountain of the Sun; the Tuareg, descendants of the Garamantians, still wear the veil; the Troglodytes still live in caves and holes of the earth, and bury their dead with laughter. Many of the ancient names have come down through the ages – such as Cydamus, now Ghadames; Garma, now Djerma; and Augile, now Augila. Even the name Hoggar, or Ahaggar, comes down from the Roman name of Mt. Uzzar.

But the Sahara is slowly dying, and with it is disappearing a romantic world. The ancient caravan trails are falling into disuse; the gold and ivory trade from the south to north is a part of the past; there are no longer slaves to be sold in Tripoli and Tunis, after being brought across the Sahara from the Sudan. Even the great salt caravans to and from Taodini and Timbuktu are becoming less and less numerous each year. I can foresee the day when the Troglodytes, the Siwans, and the veiled Tuareg will be no more.

But their dead cities remain. We shall be able to reconstruct the past by continuing the work at Carthage, at Leptis Magna, in the Oasis of Jupiter-Ammon, and in the region of the tomb of Queen Tin Hinan. Like a dream, the glories of old seem to pass before me the golden tomb of the Phoenicians at Utica, The Temple of Tanit at Carthage, the sea-encrusted amphores of Djerba, the treasure of Tin Hinan, the thousand mummies of the hill of the dead at Siwa, and the magical Oasis of Jupiter-Ammon – all seem to pass like the fading mirages of the desert land. Once more I can see the reflected ruins of solitary sentinels of the desert in the azure waters of the Syrtian seas, made famous in song by Homer and Virgil. And my mind holds pictures of mountain-enclosed Bulla-Regia, Khamissa, Dougga and Djemila; and of those silent ruins of the desert, Ad Majores, and abandoned Thala. Added to these swift moving mental panoramas are the historic lands of the Faiyum, and the rock-rimmed valleys of the great Saharan central lands.

But the pictures are fragmentary, at best, and cry out for completion. There is so much more to learn; there are so many unknown trails to follow; there is splendor and beauty and romance beneath those sands, and out of a desert dawn comes the siren song. . .

Chapter 8

THE TEMPLE OF JUPITER-AMMON

"And thou did'st shine, thou desert moon upon
All this, and cast a wide and tender light,
Which softened down the hoar austerity
Of rugged desolation, and fill'd up,
As 'twere anew, the gaps of centuries;
Leaving that beautiful which still was so,
And making that which was not, till the place
Became religion, and the heart ran o'er
With silent worship of the great of old!
The dead, but sceptred sovereigns, who still rule
Our spirits from their urns"

– Lord Byron.

It was the writings of Herodotus, that great reporter and historian of ancient times, that first put into my head the idea of exploring the Libyan Desert. Since earliest school days his wonderful descriptions of the old world had given me the desire to discover, if possible, what remained of the ancient civilization and peoples mentioned in his works. The Garamantian kingdom, the legendary Ammonians with their oracle temple of Jupiter-Ammon, the Nasamones, who were explorers of the Sahara in antiquity, the Troglodytes and Lotus Eaters – the list is long and wondrous of lost kingdoms and peoples who once lived in the land called Libya.

"There can be few tracts of the earth's surface which present such a number and variety of interesting problems as the Libyan Desert."[1] The geographical and archaeological history of this vast and little explored section is not only a field presenting interesting problems, but the last three years of scientific researches have been prolific in interesting results, especially in the Faiyum Oasis and in the region of the Oasis of Jupiter-Ammon. It may be recalled that the Geographical Review published an article in 1925 on the "Ancient Trade Routes from Carthage into the Sahara,"[2] and this chapter may serve to illustrate the great importance of Siwa, the Oasis of Jupiter-Ammon, called by Professor Gautier, "The Doorway of Two Worlds, and the Ancient Key to Egypt."

The old trail to the Oasis of Jupiter-Ammon, and to the chain of oases beyond, has been known since earliest history. From Herodotus we learn that the caravan route from Thebes on the Nile led first to the kingdom of the Ammonians, thence to Augila, Garama, the ancient capital of the Garamantians, and from there on to Carthage.

The caravan route followed to-day to the famous Siwan depression is the one used by Alexander the Great on his visit to the Oasis of Jupiter-Ammon in 331 B.C. So great was the fame of the oracle at Jupiter-Ammon in Alexander's time that the great Macedonian conqueror, flushed with his victorious conquest, decided to visit the Oracle Temple and inquire if he were not, in fact, of divine origin. It is hardly to be wondered that so brilliant a youth might find reason to believe that he was something more than an ordinary man, and it would have been stupid and improvident of the oracle to have failed to declare him a god. Oracles are supposed to be wise as was this oracle.

In planning my expedition to the famed Oasis of Jupiter-Ammon, a part of my objective was to follow, as closely as possible, the footsteps of Alexander the Great. This expedi-

---

1.   John Ball, *Problems of the Libyan Desert*, Royal Geographical Journal, July, 1927.

2.   De Prorok, Geographic Review, April, 1925.

tion was planned after the discovery of the tomb of Queen Tin Hinan in 1926. I had always wanted to study the region around Siwa, to determine, if possible, whether some of my theories could be substantiated regarding the origin of these people.

Our expedition left Alexandria with a fleet of cars of light build, heavily loaded with collapsible boats, guns, surveying instruments, moving picture paraphernalia, cameras, and a considerable commissary. For two days we followed the coast line through the ancient land of Marmorica, getting glimpses now and then of the blue Mediterranean through gaps in the lovely hills. Seventy-five miles southwest of Alexandria are the ruins of the famous basilica of St. Menas, which was discovered and excavated by Professor Kaufmann, the German, just previous to the World War.

Many old tombs and Roman watch towers are passed on the way, and in places one can see the ruins of the projected railway to Sollum, which had been planned by Abbas Hilmi, the ex-Khedive. It had been his idea to shorten the distance from Egypt to Europe by at least two days, but Africa somehow throws obstacles in the way of those who would "make it snappy."

We arrived at Mersa Matru, the ancient port of Ammonia (called Praetorium by the Romans), in the dead of night, and stopped at a rest house where we could hear the sea lapping at the steps of the ruins of Cleopatra's queenly summer cottage. This fairy spot, overgrown with amaryllis, and situated in the shade of tall palm trees, is on the edge of an azure blue sand-and-rock-enclosed bay. The whole is outlined by the high Libyan plateau, providing a beautiful, memorable picture. It is easy for one to imagine the ancient galleys landing their pilgrims on the shore of the bay prior to the long march across the desert to the Oracle Temple.

The moon still pours a golden flood on the landlocked bay where Anthony and Cleopatra sailed their perfumed galley, passing their last mortal hours together after having lost world empire at the battle of Actium. Cleopatra Celene, the beautiful daughter of the famous lovers, was perhaps born here. Her tomb is far to the West, and is called "The grave of the Roman lady." This famous and intelligent daughter of "the serpent of old Nile" lies far up in the Atlas Mountains, and beside her is the tomb of her husband, Juba II, king of Mauretania. There is a legend to the effect that Helen of Troy landed on this coast after the fall of that city and disappeared into the heart of Libya, where she became a desert queen.

While at Mersa Matru we decided it would be wise to test our collapsible boats in the beautiful lagoon prior to crossing the desert with them to the sacred isles of Lake Arachie and Zeitun. Never have I seen such varied and vivid color as the sea assumes in front of Cleopatra's palace. Sometimes it becomes so blue that the sea on the outer side of the reef seems purple black, while the waters of the bay itself, due to the different depths and the colored seaweeds, take on deep emerald greens and vivid turquoise blues. The palace of Cleopatra, queen of ancient Egypt, stands at the water's edge, where she could hear the soft rippling waves re-echoing through the marble corridors.

> "Thy shores are empires, changed in all save thee –
> Assyria, Greece, Rome, Carthage, what are they?
> Thy waters washed them power while they were free,
> And many a tyrant since; their shores obey
> The stranger, slave, or savage; their decay
> Has dried up realms to deserts."

We explored several passages under the ruins, and while picking up some ancient bits of mosaic I narrowly escaped being crushed when a part of the ceiling came crashing down. In the village we were able to purchase several bronze statuettes and pieces of jewelry that were supposed to have come from the ruins of the great queen's golden palace.[1]

We left Mersa Matru at dawn, just as the moon and stars had ceased to be reflected in the phosphorescent waters of the magic lagoons and when Aurora, with crimson lights, was moulding in bas-relief the distant horizon.

For several miles the fleet of cars climbed up through the brush to the high desert plateau that looked down on the white, gleaming roofs of ancient Ammonia. Alexander the Great must have stood on these heights as his gorgeous caravan passed by with its golden chariots, treasure laden elephants, and richly appareled and scintillating escort.

After the green, gazelle-filled slopes that form a ribbon of grass and bush along the coast, one enters the real desert, a dead, scorching, arid, desolate land. For hours we passed over long stretches of rock and sand, monotonous and dull going, with nothing to attract the eye or change the similarity of the drab surroundings. How discouraged the ambassadors and pilgrims of old must have felt when greeted by such a desolate region, yet even old Croesus of Lydia, rich beyond the dreams of avarice, bore the hardships of the scorching trail in order to consult the oases priests and their divinities.

Lysander the Spartan, old Cato, Hannibal, and many a king and pharaoh, crossed the same trail we now traverse, but by what different methods of transportation!

The legendary Hercules is said to have visited Siwa in his wanderings and that is why, perhaps, Alexander the Great wished to emulate him, for he claimed descent from the Greek hero. But even the mighty Alexander had his problems along this trail. Four days out from Mersa Matru, his water supply gave out and he and his army were in danger of dying of thirst. Due to the intervention of the gods (or possibly to natural phenomena) a great black cloud appeared

---

1.   Such an interesting field cannot be treated in the compass of a book on general exploration. The student will find this field ably covered by various authors cited in the bibliography.

out of the sky, bringing with it the necessary water to save the expedition.

This was quite enough to convince Alexander that he was either a god or highly favored by them. Later on, his entire command became lost and was saved by a flock of ravens that appeared to lead the host to the temple. Truly he was Alexander the Great! To-day, after more than two thousand years, the mountain where Alexander was lost is still called Djebel Sekunder. (Arab for Alexander.)

On our first night out from Mersa Matru we camped by a ruined mound and slept under the glittering stars, with the icy breath of the desert wind sweeping over us and chilling us to the bone. At dawn we packed hurriedly and raced along the arid "pans," flat mud basins dried hard, which made wonderful going for the cars. From the back of the leading car we filmed the trailing cars, and the pictures show hardly a quiver, so flat and smooth was the going.

We reached the great depression of Siwa at sunset, just as all the desert rocks, hills and sands became scarlet and pink, and when our shadows, outlined against the sand dunes, took on the grotesque forms of antediluvian monsters.

The first view of Siwa and the Oasis of Jupiter-Ammon is most picturesque, for after crossing the bleakest kind of desert one suddenly looks down from the vividly colored rock terraces of the high plateau into the depression where lies the mirage-like ensemble of crystal lakes reflecting the image of graceful palm trees. We stopped for a moment on the edge of the plateau to gaze with delight on the enchanting view of the oasis as seen from the edge of the colorless desert. What a joy it must have been to the pilgrims of old to catch sight at last of the promised land after the dreadful ten days' trek across the blistering sands.

We descended through wild ravines that were utterly desolate, with here and there great boulders tortured into strange forms by the chisels of wind and time. It was the hour of shadows, and the fantastic pinnacles of rock became still more weird and unearthly as we descended the canyon that led to the sea of palms.

Soon we came out of the canyon and were gliding swiftly among the softly murmuring palm trees. Night had fallen and the stars had leaped to Heaven's stage as we headed for the heart of the oasis of the ancients. Quite suddenly, it seemed, we came to the lakes and lagoons that lay shimmering under the beams of the golden desert moon. Not a breath of air stirred, and the palm-covered islands were reflected in the still waters like a pen-and-ink drawing against a background of deep violet, wherein gleamed a thousand stars. Far beyond, in gaps between the islands, we could see the sand dunes of the Libyan Desert, mellowed by the vivid moonlight and reflected in the silent waters like piles of silver dust.

We arrived at midnight at our camp on the flanks of the Djebel Muta, "The Hill of the Dead." The last I remember of that night was the thudding tom-toms beating in the direction of Siwa town – the ancient drums of the first Siwans, the last and miserable descendants of the lost Ammonian kingdom.

Siwa at last! Actually it is only about one hundred and ninety miles from the coast, but it is a world apart. The town of Siwa itself is built on a rock rising out of the plain. With its towering walls, hundreds of eye-like loopholes and many minarets, it reminds one of some mediaeval city. The present day Siwans are an unusual race with a distinct language and many strange customs.[1] They are degenerates of the lowest order, fanatical and superstitious. They are of Berber descent, and consequently are the last remnants of the ancient Libyans.

Until recent years Siwa was forbidden to Christians. The explorers of the Nineteenth Century were nearly all mal-

---

1.   See Chapter 9, "Children of the Dark."

treated or repulsed, several were killed, and few indeed reached the strangest of all strange cities of the Sahara. Though the climate of the Siwan depression is quite health-ful, the indolent population is fast dying out, and in the not too distant future only the crumbling ruins of their ancient walls and temples will remain to bear witness to the past.

Two miles south of the present town is the sacred and imposing mass of ruins of the Acropolis of Agourmi. Here we find the ruins of one of the most famous temples of antiquity. Here stood the temple of Jupiter-Ammon; here, under the tall, graceful trees, came the illustrious of the past ages to consult the mystic oracle. Here came Alexander the Great to inquire if he was indeed the son of Zeus, and here he was received with divine honor by the priests, departing even greater than he came – a living god![1]

Here, too, came Croesus, Lysander, Cato the Younger, Hannibal, great Carthaginians and pharaohs, and kings and ambassadors without number. It may be well to say here that in the neighborhood of the temple we discovered several coins bearing the image of Alexander the Great as the god of Ammon, wearing the twin horns of the sacred Ram and bearing in his hands the royal symbols of a Pharaoh of Egypt.

South of the temple, at a distance of about a quarter of a mile, is the famed Fountain of the Sun, spoken of by Hero-dotus and many other ancient historians.[2] It is the largest and most beautiful of a dozen flowing wells that fed the oasis, and it was famous in ancient times for the phenomenon of its waters being warm at night and cold in the day.

It is not easy to construct a forthright narrative of Siwa and its surrounding territory. There is so much of interest, especially to the explorer while on the field, and when writ-ing of it at some later period, that he is confronted with a

---

1.   Callithene, who accompanied, Alexander to the Oasis of Ammon. Diodorus-Sic-ulus, Herodotus I, p. 46, Pausanias III, 18.
2.   Ovid-Metam., XV, pp. 309-310. Pomponius Mela, I, 39. Pliny the Elder.

desire to advance in all directions at the same time. The fancy of the average visitor, however, would doubtless be held by the two outstanding features of the place, viz: the gruesome Djebel Muta (Hill of the Dead), and the splendid Fountain of the Sun. Opposite poles, certainly, but who can escape the charm of a living fountain, and who is free of wonder concerning those whose eyes have been closed these long, long centuries? Perhaps the proper order would be to treat the living first, and come at last to the dead, but I will reverse this order so that the reader may leave the immediate vicinity with a feeling of cleanliness and a better taste in his mouth. This procedure might well be recommended to any writer. A book, like a highway or an inviting side road, is profitless if its pleasant memories do not quite drown out the more unpleasant features.

Our camp at Siwa was actually on the dreadful "Hill of the Dead," the Necropolis of the ancient Ammonian kingdom. From our mud and palm-thatched headquarters we could see hundreds of skulls and skeletons bleaching in the glaring sunlight, or grinning evilly under the desert moon. If ever there was a place where ghosts should roam, and haunting noises be heard, it is here on Djebel Muta, where we made our home for ten weeks.

The hill of mummies is honeycombed with long dark passages, eerie caverns and bat-infested tombs. We explored endless funereal sepulchers, one leading into the other, with rows of the dead lying in their mummy wrappings and grinning sardonically down upon us from their bunk-like compartments. These mummies are particularly well preserved, the air being so dry that time fails to exact its obliterating toll. Some of the tombs have wonderful carvings and endless hieroglyphics telling of the life of the deceased, giving his name, his occupation, and offering prayers for the future world.

These prayers are teachers of hope. The explorer of prehistoric peoples is constantly faced with the proof that man, from the earliest time, has lain himself down to his long rest fortified in the belief that a better world is to come. It might be interesting for the philosopher to pursue the theory that man has always sensed a fellowship and eternal bond with the infinite.

Not all the mummies buried here have escaped disturbance. Thieves and hyenas have dragged many of them from their last resting places, and some of the more courageous Siwans have actually made their homes in the cool chambers of the forgotten dead.

It is a fearsome business, this roaming about through the caverns of the dead, armed with electric torches that serve to magnify the gruesome objects until one feels it would be better to be out in the clean fresh air. But there are beads, ancient pottery, emeralds, lapis lazuli, and countless mummy wrappings still to be found in the stifling depths of this "Mountain of the Dead," and this is quite enough to lead the explorer on. So, by the aid of electric torches and candles, we copied down the ancient symbols and inscriptions, half suffocating all the while, and fearing every moment that some chamber might cave in and bury us alive. We were always glad when evening came to relieve us from our labors and to bless us with the gorgeous spectacle of the blazing African sunset. Then, glad to be living, we would sit and listen to the moving cadence of the throbbing tom-toms coming through the clear, clean air from Siwa town.

From our headquarters on the Djebel Muta we were able to overlook all the antiquities of the historic oasis and of the region around. Southeast of the "Mountain of the Dead," through gaps in the groves of majestic pomegranate and olive trees, lies the lovely legend-surrounded "Fountain of the Sun." Let us go there now in the cool of the evening and refresh ourselves. There we can stroll beneath the palms, whose myriad fronds sift out the blue of night and shower the dark waters with the flash of heaven's jewels; there we can bathe ourselves in the healing waters of the living fountain.

Later, by a camp fire, let us listen to someone who, skilled in the art of story-telling, can catch for us a romance worthy of this setting. Let us dream a little of Alexander, of Cato, of all the wealth and splendor gathered at this place, nor be surprised when the thought comes that these same waters have reflected the images of lovers from time immemorial, and the palms, with their deep glooms, have offered them fitting sanctuaries for their whispered vows of fidelity and devotion.

As has been earlier said, this *"Fons Solis"* was already famous in the days of Herodotus, and was celebrated by ancient historians for the phenomenon of its waters being "cool in the daytime and warm at night." Our first visit to the fountain was unheralded, and as we approached the emerald pool in its setting of tall graceful palms we surprised a half dozen young Siwan maidens splashing and swimming about in the sparkling, bubbling water. They had not the slightest idea that there were any Roumi (Christians) within hundreds of miles.

It was a scene that could have been taken from a page of Greek mythology. The slim, powerful brown bodies of the maidens seemed absolutely natural to this sacred pool, which has ever been a shrine of beauty. We made a silent retreat, not anxious to disturb their joyous sports. It is really their pool (certainly at such a time), so we strolled back through the trees and flowers, listening to the laughter of these daughters of the oasis echoing through the arcades of this fairy dream-forest.

Later we had many fine swims in this old fountain, at hours when the brown water nymphs were absent. To swim in the warm waters of the Fountain of the Sun is a never-to-be-forgotten experience. The ancient foundations of the fountain are clearly seen through the green depths forty feet down, and the great volume of sparkling waters come out of a submarine world of vivid water plants that shine and sparkle as the sunlight is reflected on them from above.

There are numerous ruins in the vicinity of the fountain and we can well believe that many sacred ceremonies and stately processions passed by the pool on their way to the Temple of Jupiter-Ammon, which is situated a quarter of a mile away. It was through a gap in the groves of giant palms that we first gazed on the golden ruins of the lesser temple of the oracle.

Only a pylon remains standing – a proud, yet pathetic reminder of a glorious past never to return. The fallen stones are covered with exquisitely carved hieroglyphics, and some of these stones still retain the antiquated blue stucco, placed there centuries ago. At sunset the weather-beaten, majestic old stones take on a gloriously warm crimson tone, which provides a wondrous contrast to the green palm trees below and the clear transparent blue of the skies.

Beyond the palm-surrounded temple of the plain towers the rock citadel of Agourmi, on whose summit was built the famed temple and the palaces of the Ammonian kings and high priests. The historic citadel was built on a multi-colored sandstone pile, which towers above the plain of the oasis. To-day a few miserable Siwans live among the salt-and-mud houses that half cover and hide the temple walls and doorways.

On our first visit we were greeted at the entrance of the great door that leads up to the ruins by the Sheik of Agourmi, who escorted us through the tortuous and gloomy passages leading to the doorway of the temple. What a gorgeous sight it must have been in bygone days to witness a royal caravan of some king, with his magnificent retinue, winding up the face of the rock to consult the oracle.

We dimly imagined the procession of Ammonian high priests carrying their golden vessels. Behind them came the swaying elephants with their gorgeous trappings, carrying on their backs some mighty conqueror and his retinue of ser-

vants, lords, and men at arms. Behind them came the dancing girls with their clashing cymbals, followed by a long
train of weary pilgrims, soldiers, and slaves, footsore and
exhausted after the long trek across the desert, but driving
themselves on now with a new courage as they approach the
central temple where stood the emerald-encrusted statue of
the oracle.

Yes, here came the suffetes and soldiers of distant
Carthage on swaying elephants that rocked the world; here
came dusky kings from the Sudan, bringing their gold and
ivory; here came the ancient Libyans and Garamantians,
bringing their lapis lazuli and emeralds from the secret
mines of the Hoggar; here came white-robed Greeks, bearing their works of art; and here came the Pharaohs of Egypt,
to place at the feet of the oracle alabaster vases filled with
the jewelry of wealthy princes of the Nile.

To-day our footsteps ring hollow along the silent corridors where once trod the mighty of old. There is no blare of
trumpets, there are no outriders to advise the high priests
that a pilgrim caravan has come. Somehow we felt out of
place. How puny were our affairs; how impossible to interest the oracle in our problems. Why, here came Alexander,
young, alert, his quick eye seeking new worlds to conquer!
And having conquered all his eyes beheld, he came here to
ask this oracle if he, Alexander, were not himself a god. And
who shall say the strength of his desire did not dictate the
oracle's reply?

Fameless souls that we are! Can we gain counsel from an
oracle who saw Hannibal, the swarthy Carthaginian, come to
inquire if he could still lift up armies against his hated enemies, the Romans? Impecunious wretches that we are! How
can we hope to gain the ear of an oracle, who saw Croesus
come to lay his untold wealth at the feet of the oracle in
exchange for a word assuring him of future life? Troubled
spirits that we are! What words shall we choose to speak to
an oracle who heard the voice of Cato philosophising?

Unskilled historians that we are! What shall we say of a place that brought Herodotus here to study and to preserve for posterity some of the wonders of this famed altar of the Ammonian kings?

But the Sheik of Agourmi seems to know nothing of our lowly estate, and so with electric torches and candles we crept through the ruined passages, now and then being confronted by walls covered with inscriptions and rock carvings in Egyptian style, depicting priests and animals. Rubbish and debris of fallen walls so obstructed the citadel that it was impossible for us to determine the exact ground plan of the temple. On two or three occasions, when coming out into the daylight, we turned corners so abruptly as to come unexpectedly upon some unprepared Siwan girl who, thoroughly frightened, would disappear into some hole or crevice as quickly as would a lizard.

The old Sheik took us up to his lair on the summit of the rock, where we were forced to observe the regular Siwan custom of drinking three cups of minted tea. This is one of the invariable hospitalities of the region. The tea is sickeningly sweet, and pungent with the flavor of mint. The host first samples the concoction and then passes his cup to the guest. I have never been able to determine whether it is the flavor of the mint, the sugar, or the Sheik that I dislike most.

The view from the roof of the Sheik's house was superb. We could see the whole of the oasis with its thousands of green palms and vivid blue lagoons enclosed by the multi-colored mountains. Poor old Sheik! Surrounded by his half dozen wives, he lives squalidly amidst the ruins of faded glories and occupies the place where the treasure collecting priests of old held their deceiving rites and strange ceremonies.

The Siwans tell of many subterranean passages in the rock foundations below the ruined temples and palaces. One of these passages, they contend, leads to the "Hill of the Dead" two miles away, and another is a connecting passage leading to the Temple of the Palms in the plain below. We do know that there is a well on the great rock, a deep well that leads far into the bowels of the hill. Legend has it that half-way down this well there is a door leading to the undiscovered treasure of the Ammonian priests, who hid their wealth in the heart of the citadel.

This legend is encountered on every hand. I have no faith in it, but I do know that the place is yet a great storehouse of knowledge where much is yet to be learned. For example, consider my own good fortune in finding several ancient coins. Three of these coins bore images of Alexander the Great, crowned with a diadem of Zeus. I also found several Roman coins and one Carthaginian. All of these coins were given to the Greco-Roman Museum at Alexander, save the Carthaginian coin, which I kept.

A great page of history speaks to one from that little bronze coin, on which is depicted one of the famous horses of Numidia standing under a palm tree. It brings to mind the statement of Silius Italicus, who described Nebis, the Ammonian warrior prince, as "fearlessly and splendidly armed," riding in the army of Hannibal.

It is said that the Temple of Jupiter-Ammon was founded in 1385 B. C. There are numerous legends concerning its origin, but that of Herodotus is the most interesting. He says that the oasis temple was founded by Ethiopians. In support of this he declares that two dark girls were carried away from the Temple of Jupiter-Ammon at Thebes, one of whom founded the famous oracle of Dodona in Greece, while the other wandered into the Libyan Desert and founded the oracle of Jupiter-Ammon at Siwa. Her utterances were considered supernatural. In her we have another female half-god of the desert to join the goddess Tanit at Carthage, Queen Tin Hinan of the Hoggar, mysterious Libya, La Kahena, and Queen Dido – legend and history forever around some lady of the Sahara!

Regardless of who founded the oracle, for centuries it was a shrine, eagerly visited by pilgrims, and was considered sacred, holy ground. Pliny tells of the sacred stone at Siwa which, if touched by sacrilegious hands, would cause the dreaded sand storm to come raging out of the desert. This same superstition exists to-day in certain tribes.

The poet Pindar dedicated an ode to Jupiter-Ammon, which was kept for six centuries under the altar at Agourmi. If only we could come across it some day! Greek galleys plied regular service between Greece and what is now the port of Mersa Matru, so that the Greeks might cross the wide sea to consult the oracle. Strabo states that the sea at one time reached the temple, and bases his curious claim on the fact that considerable quantities of seashells have been found in the vicinity of the oasis!

As regards the ritualistic rites practiced here, we may safely conclude that they were similar to those employed in other oracular temples, with the central figure of the oracle depicted as dead and wrapped for burial. The statue of the god was covered with emeralds.

The old Sheik of Agourmi told us that he had found several emeralds among the ruins and had sold them to a merchant in Cairo. Whence came these emeralds is now a subject receiving a great deal of study. We spent three days trying to locate the emerald mines, said to be in the Djebel Dakrour. These lost mines have been mentioned by many mediaeval Arab historians, and their statements are sworn to by all the present-day picturesque liars of Siwa.

But it was not the wealth of Siwa that brought the famous ones of old to this oasis. There were high priests in that day wise enough to tell the pilgrims what they wanted to know. It is rather too bad that we cannot to-day consult that same oracle and learn much that is yet to be learned concerning all of the region round about. It would save years of excavation, study and patient toil. But to-day

"The oracles are dumb
No voice or hideous hum
Runs through the arched roof in words deceiving."

We must, therefore, resort to more natural means for the making of our discoveries. With this in mind it might be well to outline briefly some of the interesting fields in this immediate region, as well as give mention to some of the legends surrounding the whereabouts of dead cities, lost oases, and unmarked tombs.

South of Djebel Dakrour lie the vast unexplored regions of the Libyan Desert, indicated on the maps of to-day by an unspotted blank space of over a thousand square miles. It, too, has its interesting secrets, but it has held them through the centuries. Time after time old Siwans have told me of a lost city half buried in the sand far out in what they call "The Devil's Country." We made some exploration in that section, but we never found any traces of a buried city or "Lost Oasis," though we know they exist.

It is somewhere in this vast region that Cambyses' mighty army was lost. Using Memphis as a base, his command of fifty thousand men, under capable generals, set out to capture the Oasis of Jupiter-Ammon. They had strict orders to pillage and destroy the temple and enslave the people. But a great sand storm arose out of the desert, and the screaming, sand-laden winds blew out the life of that vast host. The Ammonians related that not a man survived after passing the Oasis of Khargeh.

Somewhere in the mournful, desolate spaces that stretch southeast of the Djebel Dakrour, lies mummified the army of Cambyses, which perished in 525 B. C. How wonderful to find something of this once mighty host, with its war chariots and armor-clad men-at-arms lying under the protecting sands of age. An old Arab historian, the dean of the Siwan sheiks, told me of two other armies that were lost in the Libyan Desert – both of which were on the way to plunder

Siwa. Quite evidently, the Siwans have a historical background for their belief that the gods smite those who come to desecrate the altar house of the Oracle of Jupiter-Ammon.

The Siwan depression is formed by a series of beautiful lakes and oases nearly one hundred and twenty-five miles in length.[1] Ruins of ancient towns are to be found all along the shores of these salt lakes, which are of a vivid deep blue color. Zeitun, Khamissa, Maraghi and Kasr-Roum are sites of ancient ruins that probably had connections with Siwa by water, as traces of stone landing quays are still to be seen.

It is rather interesting that while exploring in Siwa, we discovered among some of the subterranean passages, ancient rock drawings of boats with sails, and barges with numerous oars, similar to the ones used by the Egyptians. They must have known of their use, and employed them. However, we believe that the islands of the sacred lakes have not been visited since the days of the Ammonian kingdom.

One of the objects of the expedition was the exploration of the legendary islands of Lake Arachie, famed as the place where the fabulous treasure of Mohammed is buried, including his sword and seal. Hamliton, Browne, and a French explorer, Colonel Butin, all failed[2] to reach the island, but our specially made collapsible boats, which we carried across the desert, were successful. Though no treasure was found on the islands, we found traces of tombs cut into the rock, as well as worked flints and other evidences of human existence calling for detailed excavation this coming season.

The Siwans will tell you that Lake Arachie and its islands are cursed and haunted, and for proof will point to whirlpools in the lake. But these, we discovered, were caused by submarine wells.[3]

1. Publications of the Egyptian Geological Survey.
2. White, S., *From Sphinx to Oracle*, 1900.
3. John Ball, Royal Geographical Journal, *Problems of the Libyan Desert*, August, 1927.

The region borders on the Egypto-Tripolitan frontier, where military operations are being conducted by the Italians against the rebel tribes of Cyrenia, who had fled as far south as the deserts near Jarabub (their recently acquired oasis).

On this vague frontier, not far from the Oasis of Girgab, is the famous "Singing Dune," a vast mountain of sand dreaded by the Siwans.

While exploring this desolate desert region southwest of the Siwan depression, and in the general direction of Kufara, we located one of the richest prehistoric fields in Africa. Thousands of beautifully worked flint instruments were found on the rock terraces that in prehistoric times enclosed a series of lakes, similar to the present day Siwan agglomeration of desert-enclosed waters. It is impossible to estimate the density of the Neolithic population that must have inhabited this region, which to-day is absolutely arid and forbidding. I am convinced that primitive man lived on the desert plateau rather than in the Nile valley, for the richest sites of all epochs are found in the high desert west of the Nile (Faiyum Oasis, Abydos, Siwa, etc.).[1]

As is often the case in the Sahara, these prehistoric stations are partly covered by the great sand dunes, but nevertheless many hundreds of acres in this part of the western Libyan Desert have been spared by the slowly moving dunes. An American institution will undertake to make a special campaign of research this coming winter in this field, and it is hoped that many problems will be elucidated with regard to the origin of ancient Libyans. All prehistoric periods are represented here, from Upper Paleolithic to the Neolithic and Proto-historic.

It now seems certain that prehistoric man lived at similar epochs since earliest times along the series of depressions that reach across Africa from southern Mauretania to the

---

1.   Schweinfurth, G., *Aufnahmen in der Osflichen Wuste*, Berlin, 1902. De Prorok, *Recent Prehistoric Researches in the Sahara*, 1928.

Red Sea. The controversy with regard to the climatic changes in the Sahara seems definitely settled when one continually finds the centers of prehistoric man in the most arid and secluded regions of the great desert to-day.[1]

The problem of the sand dunes is at present another object of discussion. Several scholars are putting forward the theory that the great dune centers are stationary. This seems questionable after the discovery of so many different prehistoric sites leading under, and being covered by, the mountains of sand.[2]

The present inhabitants of the Libyan Desert are fond of tales of "lost oases," especially concerning Zenzura, "The Oasis of the Blacks," generally placed south of Siwa. They also speak of divers mysterious "lost cities" in the great unexplored regions of the western Libyan Desert. Many hours are spent, sometimes quite profitably, interviewing the old story-tellers of the different oases in regard to buried treasure, "lost oases," tombs and rock drawings.

Though the majority of our expeditions to such localities were wasted efforts (an average of one in every eight!), it was due to such information that we discovered many interesting Libyan inscriptions. A strong similarity exists between these prehistoric signs carved on the rocks of the Libyan Desert and the so-called Glozel alphabet.[3]

The Abu Moharic dunes, southeast of Siwa, are one of the strangest sights of the Libyan Desert. They stretch for two hundred and twenty miles in an absolutely straight line and are generally about half a mile in width.

Dr. John Ball, who has recently been making researches for the Desert Survey of Egypt to the sea of Siwa, has located the deepest depression in Africa at Qattara. Eleven thousand square miles are below the sea level in this region,

1.   Gsell, Stephan, *Ancient History of North Africa*. IV., 1913-27.
2.   Harding, King. *Mysteries of the Libyan Desert*, 1925. *The Nature and Formation of Sand Ripples and Dunes*. Geogr. Journ. 47. 1916, p. 189. Beadnell, *The Sand Dunes of the Libyan Desert*, Geogr. Journ. 45, 1910, p. 379.
3.   See Prorok, *Illustration*, Paris, August 18, 1928.

the greatest depth reaching three hundred and twenty-five feet below sea level!

It is hoped that the coming campaign of archaeological and geographical researches will solve some of the problems briefly sketched here, and which have already been approached. Both the prehistoric and historical fields are rich in promise. There is no doubt that Siwa, and the Oasis of Jupiter-Ammon, should afford scientific results of great importance to all interested in the historical sites and the many lost civilizations of the past.

Siwa, capital of the renowned Kingdom of Ammonians, at the Oasis of Jupiter-Ammon, lies at the crossroad and junction of the old caravan trails between Egypt and Western Africa. Here passed in review a varied series of caravans. What did they leave behind? What was their influence? How much were they in turn influenced by the contact?

Dry and dusty problems to the layman, perhaps, but high adventure and romance walk hand in hand with the work necessary to the solution of the problems presented by the greedy, obliterating desert sands.

Chapter 9

CHILDREN OF THE DARK

"But a desert stretched and stricken left and right,
left and right,
Where the piled mirages thicken under white, hot
light;
A skull beneath a sandhill and a viper coiled
inside –
And a red wind out of Libya roaring 'Run and
hide. . .'"

While camping on the "Hill of the Dead," some two miles from Siwa, word was brought to us that the people of Siwa were soon to hold their festival of Sidi Suliman – their biggest annual event. Naturally, we at once made plans to be witnesses of this unusual spectacle.

Sidi Suliman, the great Marabout of the Siwans, was a most holy man, a great Kadi, whose mighty deeds have been handed down in the endless legends and innumerable super-stitions that have arisen around his sacred memory. Every year his greatness is celebrated in a religious festival that ends in an infernal, diabolical orgy.

In front of the half-ruined battlements of the frowning walls of Siwa there is a large square. In this open space is to be found the tomb of Sidi Suliman, the patron saint of the Siwans, and it is here that the festival in his honor reaches its most fantastic heights.

Preparations for the great day are made weeks in advance. Money is saved, food is stored, and fruit is carefully washed, the women prepare tons of sweets and cakes, and – the men prepare the drinks! All Siwa is cleaned up on the eve of this glorious event. The houses are made spic and span, the walls of the buildings are newly whitewashed, while colored carpets, rugs and flag-like drapes are hung from the roofs and the windows. One day in the year Siwa is thoroughly renovated, which is considerably more than can be claimed by many African towns.

As the day of the Mulid, or festival, approaches, the suppressed excitement is at the fever point. No one thinks or dreams of anything but the feast and Fantasia. Gallons of *lubki* have been drawn from the palm trees and left to stand so that fermentation may work its magic and the drink become as potent as possible. Indeed, prayers both long and earnest are offered up that it will be so. The sheep and camels are fattened, the feast is made ready, and at last the interminable suspense is over – the day of the Mulid has arrived!

On the morning of the first day everyone dresses in his Sunday best, slicks himself up in the most approved fashion and is then ready for the church parade to the respective mosques. But the services are not long, the prayers being said in great haste.

The first meal is now on. The men eat until they can gorge no more. What is left is passed on to the ladies, who in turn pass what they leave to the servants, who gnaw the bones before throwing them to the dogs.

In the afternoon visits are paid in order to see who is giving the biggest party. The great accumulation of sweets and sticky things is a signal for all the flies from the surrounding region to gather and pay their respects to the good things. To the inexperienced onlooker it would appear that there is keen competition between the flies and the Siwans, but with the flies being the only ones conscious of the competition. In modern advertising parlance, a Siwan is not "fly conscious."

The heat is generally around 100° F., and the smell of the fruit and meat is beyond description. Every article of food is actually black with flies. Though the Siwan may treat the flies with haughty and studied indifference, he has, nevertheless, a strict code of table etiquette. Some of the following rules are laid down but not always followed:

A gentleman must never take a bite from a piece of meat and then replace it in the dish.

A diner must never turn around to see if more food is coming to the feast.

A guest must never be undecided in his choice, handling first one piece and another.

A guest must eat all that he can, extending himself to his limit, and must never be content with one helping.

No matter what is offered, it is bad taste to refuse it, and still worse to spit out the morsel after tasting it.

There are many more rules, but the civilized world will not be helped by a recital of them, especially since they can hardly be recommended to polite society.

At last the visiting and feasting of the afternoon is over. The *lubki* is now collected for the big splash. The tomb of the saint is lighted with candles and the great square is carpeted with ancient rugs and vivid carpets, the whole blending into the dark shadows of the frowning walls. Prayers are again held. Then a procession forms, headed by priests who direct the chorus of several hundred powerful male voices lifted in majestic refrain. Here before us the religion, passion, and barbaric rites of the mystic Orient are being interwoven into a senseless orgy. We are back in the dark ages! The priests of the oracle are leaving the mosques; their majestic mien and high-pitched voices hold in thrall the simpler minds of the people. As it was in the past, so it is to-day, and shall be always – the many led by the few!

A great circle is now forming. An old Sheik takes the center of the circle and begins a quiet prayer that becomes increasingly louder until at last the audience joins in, chanting the Mohammedan creed. But now the fanatical madness is coming on. Hereditary and ancient cults give to the newer religion a severe setback. The white-robed figures begin to sway back and forth like a great procession of ghosts that have come down from the "Hill of the Dead" to hold unholy carnival. The hoarse voices repeat in ever-increasing crescendo "Allah – il Allah – la-la-la," and the muffled drums begin to beat the barbaric rhythm of the desert tribes.

More and more people have crowded into the square. Lanterns and torches are now moving in and out of the tortuous passages of the winding streets; the roofs are covered with veiled women who, in their white robes, look like so many shrouded phantoms. The moon, rising above the eastern rim, casts its mellow light over the towers and canyon-like walls of this weird city of the desert.

Now the dance is beginning in the great square. Several groups are formed, the drums are beginning to beat in louder tones and the flutes pierce the desert air with their mystic wailing. The clashing cymbals drown the voices of the chanting multitude. Great caldrons are beginning to seethe over glowing embers; the women are gathering on the outskirts of the crowd, bringing earthenware braziers, from which pour clouds of incense. The distant gardens are now illuminated with a thousand dancing lanterns, as if thousands of fireflies were winging erratic flight among the palm and pomegranate trees.

> "And the fireflies in the dark night
> Drift around like dust of starlight
> Till on beams of wanest moonlight
> They are wave-like swept away."

Now from the groves comes the sound of singing as wild and savage as though all the demons of the lower region were suddenly let loose upon the earth. The surging dancers in the center of the square begin beating cadence with their hands. Slowly the din becomes more ear-splitting. The drums are lashed into a continuous roar; the frenzied, naked dancers career round and round, drinking the wildly maddening *lubki*. To our surprise our own negro servant, Mohammed, suddenly takes the center of the ring, flourishing a jug of *lubki* as he wheels and pivots in drunken frenzy.

As the night progresses the orgy envelops the multitude. More and more drinks are supplied; more and more devil dancers come from the sacred groves, carrying torches and brandishing them above their heads. Thousands of sparks fly right and left from the flourished torches.

All Siwa is now raving mad. The screams and yells of the hysterical dancers add to the crescendo of clamor caused by the dreadful clashing of the drums. The air is filled with swirling eddies of incense, and the light of the blazing torches falls on glistening black flesh and gleaming eyes. Leaping fires cast the shadows of the demon dancers against the walls of the citadel, magnifying the weird and eerie scene into an unbelievable phantasmagoria.

The scene now becomes too degenerate to describe. The cults of the dead gods are alive again; Tanit, Baal and Moloch hold sway once more! Through the ages they have been kept alive by the hidden fires of passion, forever ready to burst forth in the bodies of these uncivilized children of the desert.

Siwan Customs

It is not the author's purpose to here set out a fulsome encyclopedia of Siwan customs. To do so would be to make certain the suppression of the book. Beyond question, Siwans are the most degenerate people in all the world, but certain of their customs are of interest and can be briefly outlined without fear of giving offense.

Africa has always been the land of superstition and of the dark arts. The Sahara is the home of the dreaded Djenoun of the Tuareg; it is the home of the Djinns of the Arabs; the dwelling place of the Shetans, Afrits and Ghuls of the Siwans. I have seen medicine men in the dark caverns of the Troglodytes; I have looked upon devil-be-witched souls in the Hoggar; I have seen strange old witches in the abandoned parts of the upper ruins of Siwa town. A considerable number of these old witches live apart in the older ruins of Siwa. They are ancient creatures, horrible to look upon, with dyed red hair and with skin not unlike that of the mummies found in the Djebel Muta. These toothless old hags, held in awe by all the Siwans, are employed to keep away evil spirits, to locate stolen goods and to concoct love phials and potions. Like the werewolves of old, these half human creatures are supposed to climb down the battlements and crawl among the tombs of the dead, where they tear off the head and carry it in their mouths to their dens in the summit of the hill.

Superstitious as is the Siwan, he knows how to turn his superstition to good account. In this connection, I shall never forget an eclipse of the moon which occurred while we were at Siwa, and the startling effect it had upon the people. As said in the preceding chapter, our camp was built on the lower slopes of the Djebel Muta. From there we could overlook Siwa. On this night we were enjoying a quiet smoke amid the tombs of the Djebel Muta, and watching the shooting stars that make the Libyan night a continual celestial entertainment. Slowly the moonlight faded. On looking up we noticed that a rim of the moon was being covered. Idly we watched the not unusual phenomenon of the heavens. A Siwan, who had been playing soft melodies on his reed flute in the shadows of the nearby palm trees, left off quite suddenly and a moment later from out of the shadows came his startled "Ya Salam" – the Siwan equivalent of Ye Gods, By Jove, Golly, and Gee Whiz, all rolled into one.

"He does not like this," Captain Hillier remarked, puffing away on his pipe.

We were sitting in the shadows, making ourselves a little more comfortable by utilizing a pile of mummy wrappings to make the rock a little softer. As the eclipse progressed we began to hear wailing and the beating of tom-toms in Siwa. Ali-Ford, Senoussi, our priceless major-domos, and Mohammed, our cook, came up to us in panic to ask if we could do something about it.

"Get out!" Captain Hillier ordered, as he struck a match, rather irreverently, I thought, on the nearby skull of a dead Ammonian. "You know perfectly well that we can do nothing about this eclipse and you may tell your friends so. We have too little gin left as it is."

For the time being I was mystified by the last remark, but presently out of the darkness we perceived a deputation coming from the village. The wailings and the beating of tom-toms had increased in volume; the panic-stricken women were emitting the wails so characteristic of mourning women wherever they are found in Africa. The whole thing was nerve racking and unearthly; we had as well be dead and visiting the lower regions.

We climbed down from our vantage point on the hill, stumbling now and then over some of the many mummies and skulls that cover the gruesome ground. It is strange how accustomed one becomes to skeletons and mummies. I think it was Silva White who, in his interesting volume, "From Sphinx to Oracle," said: "There is nothing so palpably dead as a mummy no, not even a drowned policeman!" At night the mummies on the Djebel Muta appear more gruesome than in the daytime and my wife confessed that she could never quite get used to the skulls gleaming so evilly in the moonlight.

As we moved down toward our camp we were met by the Siwans. At sight of us, all of them began jabbering and gesticulating. Clearly they thought it was all our fault, and for a moment it looked as if the evil days of "down with the Christian" were to be repeated. My thoughts at once turned to the Englishman, Browne, who, in disguise, visited the Oasis of Siwa in 1792 and was driven half way back to Egypt by outraged Siwans who followed him and pelted him with stones and rotten fruit. I thought, too, of Hornemann, who was "heralded out of Siwa by an army of braying asses – human and animal." And I suddenly remembered Hamilton, who was held prisoner in one of their houses for six weeks and was continually pelted with mud and dirt. Truly these are charming people!

Captain Hillier, who had treated them during the war with a taste of machine guns and drumhead courts-martial, told them that all was well and that cocktails would be served immediately. To my amazement he actually served them with several tins of our gasoline, which they drank with the greatest relish, saying that Christians certainly knew how to fix up good drinks! They were soon quite hilarious and had forgotten all about the eclipse if indeed they could really see it. They promptly decided to indulge in a great fantasia in front of our camp and they went through their idiotic gyrations until an early hour in the morning. Then, with drums beating, the happy and uproarious dancers returned home, singing the Siwan counterpart of "For He's a Jolly Good Fellow," or "We Won't Go Home Until Morning." I feel sure that they offered up prayers for early and frequent eclipses.

Our servants at Siwa employed many unique tricks to escape labor, and it was one of these tricks that brought to our attention another peculiar Siwan custom. One day three of our servants, Ali-Ford, Senoussi and Mohammed disappeared and were not to be found during the entire day. That night they calmly told us that they had been in hiding because "a widow was abroad." Although knowing nothing more than what they said, I promptly forgave them, and wondered if their actions might not be recommended to certain unsuspecting males in more enlightened communities. But I questioned them and brought to light the following custom:

When a Siwan dies, his widow goes into mourning for a period of forty-five days. She is said to be "Ghrula" (in mourning). During the period of mourning (I cannot believe that she is in grief, for certainly she has never received kindness and love from the hands of her husband) she remains in strictest seclusion, wailing and heaping ashes on her head. The last day of her sorrowing is completed by taking a bath at a certain spring. The worst calamity and omen of bad luck that could possibly befall a Siwan would be to meet the distressed lady when she is on her way to the well. To prevent such calamitous happening, a special Town Crier makes his way through the town on the preceding day, announcing in a loud voice that on the morrow Mrs. So-and-So will go to the well to complete her mourning. Siwan boys also go through the town, warning all that on the morrow a Lady Godiva act is to be staged, and woe betide any peeping Tom!

On the following morning no man stirs from his domicile. The doors are closed and barred. Everyone goes in hiding, except, of course, the widow, who was never less in hiding since the day of her birth. After she has finished her long deferred ablutions at the well, she returns home, where she begins hoping and praying for a new husband.

It was just such an occurrence that had caused the disappearance of our servants, and when the day had passed and they again showed themselves it was with rejoicing that they had escaped seeing the widow, for had they seen her most certainly the curse of the Evil Eye would have fallen upon them!

The Evil Eye plays a heavy role in the lives of the superstitious tribes of Africa. I recall the customary mad scamper of the women of Siwa, Agourmi, and Maraghi, to get out of sight whenever we appeared. We, as Christians, most certainly had the Evil Eye. We had only to look hard at an object to put that object under suspicion. Personally, I had been of the opinion that most of the members of our party had "mild and magnificent eyes," and while admitting myself held in thrall by my wife's eyes, had never considered her possessed of the Evil Eye. But she never could get a chance to look at a Siwan baby. The mother, upon my wife's approach, would quickly cover up the child in order to protect it from the calamitous misfortune that would be certain to follow, should she see it.

There are countless charms used by Siwans to ward off the Evil Eye, but the best charms are those made by the witches. The more difficult they are to obtain, the more efficacious are their influences. The most sought for are such charming concoctions as scorpions, human bones, mummy wrappings, finger nails, snakes' blood, intestines, bits of the Koran, toad skins and other unspeakable objects all ground together in an unholy mess. I dare say even the Evil Eye would be repulsed by such a putrid concoction.

How different is the treatment of the women of Siwa in comparison with their more fortunate sisters of the Tuareg tribes. In Siwa the women are but chattels and slaves. They are to be had at a fixed price, a price somewhat less than that of a goat or donkey. Due to their precarious position (being subject to divorce without a day's notice) they are not fond of bearing children and strong practices are performed to prevent childbirth. Browne, in 1792, first made mention of the fact that Siwan women took newborn infants, generally girls, to the top of the battlements of the town and there cast them to the street below. This custom still prevails to some extent.

However, there is always a great feast and rejoicing upon the birth of a male child, and one of the strange features of the banquet is that earth is offered the guests as a delicacy. This edible clay, of yellowish color, is mined near Jarabub. It tastes like nothing else on earth! Another essential item for the banquet is fish, and it will not be difficult for the reader to imagine the toothsomeness of the article when it is recalled that the fish has been brought across hundreds of miles of desert. It really advertises itself!

A rather interesting custom, from a medical standpoint, is the manner in which childbirth is aided. When the critical period arrives, the "doctor" creeps up behind the unsuspecting victim with an old-fashioned, cannon-like pistol. The shock of the sudden explosion – the gun being held close beside the woman's ear – is supposed to be a considerable aid in the successful addition to the population of Siwa.

Girls of Siwa are given in marriage at the age of seven, eight, and nine. We saw one bride of nine nothing more than a dear little child. Such things sicken one, and I shall speak no more about it. Anyone seeking material for a sensational book on customs, morals and manners, could visit Siwa with considerable profit – if there be real profit in such things. Although I confess to being an explorer and intensely interested in excavations, I prefer to do my digging in nice, clean dirt. It is enough to say that the Siwans are the most degenerate human beings to be found in all Africa.

The price of a bride at Siwa is about five dollars. It makes no difference whether she be old or young, rich or poor, beautiful (?) or ugly, the price remains the same. The Siwan groom is not supposed to have seen his bride, which would indicate that they are more reckless gamblers than we of the civilized world. But, as a matter of fact, his hazard is not great, for divorce in Siwa is quite as popular as in Paris or New York and is, if possible, somewhat easier and less troublesome. A man of Siwa who can boast of a dozen divorces, is an object of awe and is something of a "man about town."

Divorce lawyers will do well to stay away from Siwa, however, for their services are not the least required. According to Mohammedan law, a wife may be divorced by her husband in a most simple and direct manner. The husband merely calls in two witnesses, and in the presence of these witnesses and his wife, repeats three times, "I divorce thee." Rather simple.

I never could understand why he should be required to say it three times, unless the theory of the thing is that he may become conscience stricken along about the second utterance, or may remember what good cakes she can make and decide to try to worry along a little longer.

After the Siwan has divorced his wife, his witnesses are then invited to a cup of tea. Over the tea cups they enter into the discussion of such important things as the weather and the crops.

As has been said, girls marry between the ages of seven and nine, so that a girl of eleven or twelve may have been divorced two or three times. It is really quite difficult to keep tab on whose wife Mrs. So-and-So is at the moment. In fact, only an experienced Parisian can ever hope to become really good at it.

While at Siwa we attended a wedding and it became my sad duty to later console the bridegroom with gasoline and gin. Poor chap! He had never seen his bride. My wife had seen her, and had taken a photograph of her, so that we went to the wedding with the dreadful secret locked in our hearts. I longed to draw the poor chap to one side and advise him to put that five dollars on another bet. But I was powerless in the matter, feeling that it is not the province of wedding guests to offer belated advice.

It was the bridegroom's first wedding, and it seemed a tough break. He was a likeable, though somewhat melancholy fellow, and I found myself feeling quite sorry for him. I am sure that he will use his influence to bring about a change in the custom of not allowing the bridegroom to see what he is getting. My only consolation in the matter of my own duplicity is that I left him a tin of gasoline as a wedding present, so that he could not cry out "Is there no balm in Siwa?" I suppose he became highly volatile.

The children of Siwa, though poor, often sickly, and always covered with flies, are dear little tots. Their very distress increased our affection. They have one day each year when they are supremely happy. This is the tenth of January, when they have what corresponds to our Christmas. On that gala day all the roofs of the houses, where there are children, are covered with palms. At night rows of torches, soaked in oil, light up the walls. The turrets and battlements of frowning old Siwa Town are turned into fantastic castles brought straight from fairyland. Under the flickering flames of the torches the strange architecture casts fantastic shadows, rising and falling, moving back and forth, so that the town becomes as a grotesque stage effect of some "Never-Never Land."

The next day the little boys and girls are attired in clean, white robes and they exchange gifts of nuts, fruits and sweets from their Christmas trees – which in this case are palms. The little tots of Siwa look forward to this day of gifts, fireworks and songs with the same eager expectancy as do their parents to the terrible feast of the Mulid. Alas! that these dear little creatures should be brought up to become victims of such dreadful orgies and bitter life. I cannot escape the feeling that we so called Christians are remiss in our obligations to our fellow men, especially when I consider that a few thousand dollars would save the lot!

The people of Siwa live, in the main, on the product of their palm trees. The date is their staple food. The famous giant Sultana dates, that are supposed to make the Siwan women voluptuous, come from this beautiful oasis.

The palm wood enters into the construction of the houses – the dwellings being made of mud, salt and palm wood – and the palm also brings them fans, fuel, paper fibre, rope, troughs, water pipes, dykes, wine, resin, oil and sugar. Small wonder that the Siwans call their palms "an emerald bud in a circlet of gold."

The oldest records of ancient civilizations tell of the proper cultivation and regulation for the upkeep of the palm. The peoples of antiquity made it a sacred emblem. The out-stretched hand, which we uncovered on the altars of the Temple of Tanit, had its origin in the palm. The Romans used it as an emblem. The Greeks named the Phoenicians from the word Phoenix, coming from palm. To-day it is still a decorative emblem with us. Certain United States coins bear a wreath of palms, and it is to all Christian nations the emblem of peace and of glory.

Peace and glory! What an incongruous thought in connection with vile, God-forgotten Siwa! If ever a town stood in need of the civilizing influences that have ever followed the message of the Prince of Peace, it is Siwa. We came here as explorers and as students of the past, but we left with the feeling that Siwa stood not so much in need of study as of mercy.

What the Christian religion could accomplish with these children of the dark, could they be led to accept it, I dare not predict. But I do know that they need the physical blessings that can be given them by men of science; they need a thousand and one things which we might give them without the slightest sacrifice; they need a few crumbs from the rich man's table!

Chapter 10

Sacred Lakes of the Libyan Dessert

"A tideless, dolorous, midland sea,
In a land of summer and gold and ruin."

Using Siwa as our headquarters, we explored the surrounding oases for several hundred miles. To the east lies a
series of beautiful lakes over which tower a great rock formation that reaches to the Nile, more than four hundred
miles away. As we know that the caravans of old passed this
way coming from Thebes and Memphis, we spent many
days exploring the lonely, silent canyons and the abandoned
oasis of El Arig. On the top of a sentinel-like mountain,
Captain Hillier and I discovered a strange monument in
which twelve tombs were built out of great slabs of rock. It
made us think of the tomb of Queen Tin Hinan, so many
thousands of miles away, and we considered it a strange
coincidence that the mountain was called Um Achmar, (The
White Mother) doubtless a local female divinity of old.

Northeast of the oasis of the Zeitun, about a hundred
miles, is the Oasis of Gara, or Um Es Soghier, "The Little
Mother," also probably named after some female deity. Not
far from the well of Zeitun, on the lake of Karasheid, a
ruined city was found and excavated by the ex-Khedive
Abbas Hilmi several years ago. It is said that he carried
away many camel loads of "antikas" but though one often

sees this gentleman wandering around Monte Carlo and Deauville, no scientific data is to be gotten from him regarding this last expedition to sack the Oasis of Jupiter-Ammon!

At Qattara, about eighty miles northeast of Gara, the Egyptian survey had just located the greatest depression below sea level in Africa, 450 feet below the Mediterranean. In the past there was a great inland sea here, and many geologists hold the view that a branch of the Nile passed through this region to the sea.

One day, while exploring the ruins of the old Ammonian cities along the vivid blue lakes east of Siwa, our way led through the swamps bordering the water. Suddenly a sharp pain shot through my leg. In a few moments my foot swelled to such an extent that the removal of my boot became a difficult and painful operation. A small wound, similar to one that I had once contracted in Mexico, was bleeding rather profusely. Doubtless, I had been bitten by a snake, and our one desire was to get back to camp where I could be dosed with whiskey to counteract the poison – a questionable treatment, from a medical standpoint, but not entirely barren of virtue. We knew there was a local doctor at Siwa, and it seemed prudent to consult him at once, for such local doctors have a considerable experience in dealing with cases of snake bite.

Pending his arrival, however, it was thought best to try the whiskey, of which a goodly supply was on hand at the camp. The patient, without undue protest, drank off half a bottle at once, so that when the Egyptian doctor arrived the sufferer was in a hilarious state. Instead of talking about the snake wound, I immediately started to promise the doctor, who spoke a little German, that I would make him the greatest doctor in Egypt if he would locate for me the tombs of the lost Ammonian kings! It seems that I completely mystified the worthy man in six different languages, and became so involved, linguistically, that the poor doctor left, completely baffled and amazed at this new after-result of a snake bite.

After being laid up several days, due to the excessive power of good old Scotch spirits provided by the army officers, the inflammation in the wound disappeared and we continued our exploration, taking in the regions around Siwa, especially the great tomb-filled valleys of Jirba and Gagub, which provide one of the most amazing spectacles of all these mysterious Saharan surprises. To-day the valleys are silent and abandoned, but the rocks are pierced with innumerable tombs cut into the towering precipices, many of them in such impregnable positions that it is difficult to understand how the dead were carried to such inaccessible final resting places.

Time after time we climbed like flies over the precipices where the Ammonians had buried their dead, and often we found tombs beautifully sculptured from the solid rock. We saw many paintings on the walls of the tombs that still retained mummies scenes depicting strange sacred rites, funeral ceremonies and painted figures of forgotten gods. How melancholy these abandoned oases are! strange, savage, and with their silence broken only by the winds that moan through canyons bordered by precipitous limestone cliffs.

We climbed the legendary mountain of the Siwans, Mount Khamissa, which takes its name from an Ammonian queen that ruled the land long ago. The enormous table mountain is nearly perpendicular on all sides, but a narrow mounting ridge enables one to reach the summit. This sun-painted mountain contains thousands of tombs. In a far distant past a prehistoric people dwelt here. We examined many of these half ruined rock dwellings and collected the flints that lay in their vicinity.

Southeast of Mount Khamissa, the remains of an early Christian church is half buried in the sands. It dates, probably, from the period when the first monasteries were founded on the banks of the Nile and in the Wadi Natrun.

The Siwans showed us two mounds at the base of Mount Khamissa, and also pointed out a great rock that seemed lightly balanced on a precipice above. They told us that the rock would fall some day and that on whichever of the mounds it fell it would surely indicate the legendary spot where Queen Khamissa's treasure is supposed to be buried. There are ruins of numerous tombs, houses and temples near the lovely oasis named after this forgotten queen. In one of the tombs we found a perfectly preserved mummy, a baby which could only have been a few months old at its death, a pathetic reminder that mothers have known sorrow and heartache since the dawn of time.

North of Khamissa we located a vast "pan," a depression that had once been a neolithic prehistoric site where we found innumerable worked flints sculptured into the finest of forms. In a distant valley we found the remains of a Capsien and Chellean site that promised an important field of future research. While exploring this region alone on foot, I had the strange experience of being followed all day by that ominous bird of the desert, the rapacious vulture. For hours he flew just above me, as if waiting for something to happen, and I admit to the creepy apprehensious feeling that is not unusual when one is wandering alone in the desert.

Whilst filming the islands of Lake Khamissa I nearly disappeared in quicksand but succeeded in gaining hard ground by a herculean effort only to find that the camera man had made the most of my distress by grinding out a humorous film. A similar adventure in the desolate and treacherous regions of the same lake nearly cost us one of our precious cars.

The uninhabited oases of Gagub, Melfa and Exabia are all ancient centers of civilization, as is evidenced by the thousands of tombs hidden away in the wonderful rock precipices. While on the way to Lake Arachie, to explore the legendary islands, we passed great circular mounds containing numerous flints indicating that these mounds were prehistoric defenses. Our first view of Lake Exabia, (Arachie) was most surprising. A wind dappled surface of turquoise blue waters came suddenly to view through a grove of palm trees in the midst of a mournful region enclosed by vast sand dunes and melancholy canyons. The waters of the sacred lake were as vivid as it is possible to imagine – an expanse of rippling waters set in a great circle of silver-golden sand dunes. We slowly made our way around the lake with our fleet of cars, completely fascinated by the unbelievable blue of the transparent waters.

As we crossed into Tripolitan territory we perceived several islands, floating like mirages in the heart of the legendary lake. To get a better view we climbed the wild rock pinnacles that tower about Lake Exabia. To our surprise we found a large region of silex on the plateaux above the quarry, the factory of thousands of flints we had seen in the prehistoric region of that now abandoned desert land. We tried to visualize the men of the stone age working their flints into useful forms in this prehistoric factory – the breaking off of the silex with mighty blows, the fashioning of the hard stone into the delicate forms of the implements that now lie strewn over the region, instruments that were utilized in that day for hunting, fighting and the removing of flesh from animal bones.

The beautiful lakes, circled by green and yellow palms, must have been a kind of Utopia in those dawn days. Primitive man probably lived on the islands as did their contemporaries, the lake dwellers of Switzerland – using piles and stakes to lift their thatched houses several feet above ground, a primitive but effective defense against wild beasts, snakes and other unwelcome visitors.

We explored the islands with more success than did Colonel Butin and Browne, who nearly lost their lives in the mysterious whirlpool that we located between the mainland

and one of the larger islands. Although we did not find the sword and seal of Mohammed, or the other fabulous treasure supposed to be buried there, we did find a number of prehistoric flints and traces of ancient tombs. The strangely carved stones, which we found on one of the islands, may have been the remains of a temple, but the semitropical growth was so dense on some of the islands that it was difficult to penetrate into them, and they are still well guarded by the snakes so famous in Siwan legend as protectors of the treasure. These venomous guardians reminded us of a certain tomb which we had excavated in the southeast part of the Hoggar, where under each stone lay concealed one of the poison-dealing scorpions of the desert.

From our boat we could see the haunted whirlpool, which in fact is a submarine well, throwing up volumes of water in the heart of the lake. Strange plant life is to be seen in the limpid waters, and many fish passed in and out of the clear depths, their scales scintillating in the opalescent waters like flashes of silver.

What a magic, lovely region it is, with islands that seem to float in the quiet waters which reflect the still palm trees and the high floating clouds. The sand dunes of the Libyan desert reach down to the water's edge, seemingly great masses of silver and gold suspended between a vivid blue sky and the still more vivid blue water. The whole region is so lovely that it seems unreal. The silence is like that of the Arctic wastes and the only sign of life is the arrival from time to time on the lake's edge of flocks of graceful gazelles.

It was while returning across the lake that we heard for the first time "the singing dune," a startling and weird phenomenon. Captain Hillier, hardy, unemotional Saharan that he is, was greatly disturbed by the strange sounds that swept across the still, mirage-like lake. The singing sands at last! I had heard their moan and whisper across the grim wastes of the Erg Oriental. They had blinded and choked me on many a lonely trail, but never before had they spoken to us as they did in that mysterious sunset hour on the shores of Lake Exabia.

The Siwans hold this mountain in horror, never camp within miles of it, and always race their donkeys at top speed if passing anywhere near it. The great silence emphasizes this strange phenomenon, which is caused by the wind rubbing together millions of particles of sand. It produces a sound impossible to describe. These singing sands, as well as all echoes, are abhorred by the desert folk. To them it is the voice of the dreaded Djinns – a warning of death or calamity.

I remember the King of the Hoggar telling me how the echoes in the mountains mocked him most wickedly. "They were," he said, "most impolite and were continually answering me back!"

The Tuareg says, "Where there is an echo there is also a demon!" I remember the consternation of our faithful Siwan servant, to whom we gave the name Ali-Ford (for the reason that he drove one) when we told him we would camp near the singing dune. His horrified expression was genuine, and he predicted the most calamitous consequences.

We climbed the haunted mountain, we photographed it, we slept in the neighborhood of it, but we did not again hear the eerie sounds that had come floating across the lake to us. We left the sacred lake at sunset, paddling across the waters, "A painted ship upon a painted ocean."

The spectacle was awe-inspiring as the dying sun caressed the giant mountains of sand with ever-changing colors. As swiftly as the varied tints transformed the pinnacles and curves of the dunes into pictures of loveliness they were reflected in the glassy surface of the mirror-like waters of the lake. The whole scene becomes a magic canvas slowly changing colors; lake, mountains, palm grove and sand dunes passed from vivid lights into the purple shadows of the Saharan night, and a scene that must resemble some corner of Paradise passed into memory.

We returned to camp among the prehistoric fortifications to talk and to dream about these "Islands of the Blessed," and to voice our wonder of the phenomenon of the singing sand dune.

The following day we explored the encampments of early man on the edge of the chain of desolate sand hills that lie in the great valley that leads from Siwa to Jarabub, "The Gateway of the Sahara." Through here passed the ancient caravans to and from the West, as they are still doing to-day. Here, according to Sallust, the Medes and Syrians passed on their way to Mauretania, and an army from Carthage, composed of Garamantians, Nasamones and Lusitanians, marched through here on their way to capture Thebes. Roman legionaries, Numidian cavalry, and later the veiled Tuareg, marched along this historic trail into the night of history. We found several Roman and Egyptian amphores, broken relics of some pioneer caravan of travelers who, centuries ago had passed on their way across the rocky trails of the melancholy canyon.

Southwest of the highest depression in the pass we penetrated into the "Regions of the Devil," where a thousand miles of the unknown lie before one. *Terra incognita!* How that feeling has always thrilled one – unknown horizons ahead, lost oases, mysterious hidden desert cities of which the story tellers love to tell in the market places from Siwa to Timbuktu. Soon there will be few places on the earth's surface still untrodden by man! In Africa we have still a thousand miles of ancient Mauretania to be traversed and another thousand miles southwest of Siwa. Some day, however, the Sahara will hold no more secrets, no more romantic, unblazed trails or unknown sand-buried cities, and the romance of exploration in that land will have passed forever.

The wind and sand have played strangely with the rocks of this "devil's land." Continual erosion at the bases of the boulders have made them look like giant mushrooms, very useful umbrella-like protectors from the sun during a mid-day rest.

For scores of miles we followed a chain of depressions to the south, regions of dried-up lakes on whose dim shores dwelt "the forgotten people." Never have I seen such beauti-fully worked flints as we found in the lee of the snow-like sand mountains of the western Libyan desert. These flints were of all colors and of all forms, so beautifully worked that we could but marvel at the handiwork of those early peoples. Hundreds of delicately chipped, needle-like flints were recovered here, yet what they could have been used for it is difficult to say. Some of the spearheads were a vivid cornelian-like flint; others were of a deep blue or like old amber; some were jet black and others blood red – and never two quite alike. They were superior to any flints I had seen in the Faiyum or in South Sahara, and I am now convinced that the Faiyum neolithic civilization came from the regions southwest of the Oasis of Siwa.

Though I have visited the paleolithic and neolithic cities of the Nubian desert, none compare in quantity with this region, in the heart of the most desolate part of the Libyan Desert. It is difficult to know the history of this civilization, but it is probable that they were the descendants of the earli-est primitive men, whose traces have been found in recent years in the northern part of the Sahara. The relics of man of the early stone age that I have seen from the Atlantic to the Red Sea, across the whole of North Africa, certainly indicate that the cradle of humanity could have been here.

With Professor Bovier-Lapierre I visited the great allu-vial deposits with their paleolithic stratifications on the ter-races of the Nile. Together we found specimens of this ancient Chellean civilization in the Libyan Desert, and I have seen examples of their primitive implements in the region of Siwa, Southern Tunisia and in deepest Sahara. The Chellean man has been placed by competent authorities as dating back to three hundred thousand years before Christ,

so that the Challossian man of the Sahara must date far earlier. It is my hope to some day locate the skeletal remains of
these pre-Chellean men, corresponding to the first intergla-
cial period (Gunz and Mindel) of Europe.

Numbers of neolithic remains are also to be found in the
Saharan regions similar to those found in Rhodesia. It is my
opinion that after long and patient systematic exploration of
Mauretania, the Saharan Atlas, and the Hoggar Mountains,
traces of the much-hoped-for Pliocene man will be found in
these little known regions.

Competent geologists have claimed that the Nile, or a
branch of that river, passed through the Libyan Desert west
of its present course in Pleistocene times and that this may
account for the richness of prehistoric remains in the eastern
and western Libyan regions. Primitive man has always
sought the water's edge, so that it is natural that we saw
dwellings among the caves and along the terraces of rivers
and lakes. The *"abri sous roche,"* that I found near the
Faiyum Oasis, above the ancient Lake Karun, is an example
of this, as are the cities found along the dead rivers of the
Sahara and in southwest France (where I conducted excavations at Le Moustier, in the Dordogne, during the summer
months when Africa is nearly impossible, due to the great
heat).

If the Nile passed through the Libyan Desert, it is possible that it passed through the chain of Siwan oases, and the
region has the appearance of being worn by a great river in
the past. Certain it is that the now dried up pans and depressions found in the great prehistoric region southwest of Siwa
were chains of lakes, for we found worked flints on all the
terraces as well as on all the shores of the dried up lakes and
rivers. With the changing of the course of the Niger River,
south of the Sahara, the Nile to the East, and the Igharghar in
the center, with the consequent drying up of the vast lakes in
the Libyan Desert, Southwest Hoggar (Djouf) and Southern
Tunisia and Algeria, the Shotts Djerid and Melghir, I think

we have the reason why the Sahara has "gone dry." Once the Niger, due to the heavy silting of its sands, turned its course south of the Djouf it caused the desiccation of a great inland lake similar to the present day Lake Chad, which in turn took the moisture from the Hoggar Mountains. This caused the drying up of the once vast Igharghar, which with the Oed Mia fed the once inland lakes of South Algeria and Tunisia. Lake Chad is now rapidly drying up and will soon make all this region desert land.

After mapping and surveying this prehistoric region, which we named the "Siwanien Civilization," we turned northeast to investigate the region between Lake Shiyata and Maraghi. On a mountain here, while searching for an inscription that a Siwan claimed he had seen, I discovered on the summit of the hill what appeared to be a sacrificial site. It was similar to several others that I had seen, notably the sacrificial rock outside of the cave of Fond de Gaum in the Dordogne. A cup had been carved out of the rock with a duct (for the blood) leading into it. Several hands and the outline of feet had been carved around this undoubtedly sacred spot.

We can only imagine what strange and terrible sacrificial rites took place on this mountain in the dim ages of the past! We do know that the Libyans and Carthaginians sacrificed their children by the thousands to their goddess, Tanit, for at Carthage we uncovered nearly six thousand sacrificial urns in three years of excavation, all of the urns containing the bones of little children offered up in barbaric sacrifice. Herodotus tells us that sacrifices were common among the ancient Libyans. Even to this day the Berbers of Siwa make sacrifices to appease the wrath of the gods.

When the terrible influenza epidemic of 1918 nearly wiped out the Siwans, they sacrificed a bull at the sacred tomb of Sidi Suliman. They covered the animal with wreaths of flowers and, accompanied by the music of cymbals, pipes and drums, led the beast to the altar, just as did their ancestors in the preceding ages. I have heard it whispered in Siwa that a child was made away with not long ago in one of those dread ceremonies. Certainly superstition still envelops the people of the Aures, Matmatas and Libyan deserts.

We became quite provoked with the Siwan who could not locate the stone bearing the Roman inscription that he said had lain for so long on the summit of this sacrificial mountain. He told us that the Italians at Jarabub, across the frontier, were very interested in "Kitab" writing and that probably they had come and taken it off. If so, well and good, but I fear it is lost forever.

I recall an important inscription, found at Siwa, which was being used by a Sudanese woman as a meat block! In due time she would have worn away the history-telling characters. It was the first Greco-Roman inscription to be found at Siwa. I had it sent to Doctor Braccia, the director of the Greco-Roman museum at Alexandria, for on it was engraved the name of that mighty traveler, the Emperor Hadrian, and it may lead to the discovery of other precious inscriptions that will give us light on the history of the oases and temple of Jupiter-Ammon.

To the North of Maraghi we explored a mountain that was covered with ancient inscriptions and symbols, prehistoric Libyan, Ammonian and Tifinar or Tuareg. Here we found a link with the regions two thousand miles away; the footprints carved into the rock at Maraghi were identical to those of Tiritimin and the "Love Mountain" of Merjouma! Here was proof that the great Tuareg empire stretched as far as the Libyan Desert, the inscriptions being identical with those of the Hoggar and belonged to two periods, the earliest and the later known Tifinar scripts.

"Inscription Mountain," as we called this place, had certain signs and symbols that appeared neolithic, then came others of the Lybico-Phoenician type similar to that found at Dougga, (400 B. C.) and now in the British Museum.

Some of the symbols and letters remind one of that unknown language, the inscriptions of which were discovered by Duveyrier at Ghadames and which I have seen in different parts of the extreme south of Tunisia. They were also seen on the outer wall of the tomb of Queen Tin Hinan, and at Djerma by H. Barth. It is probably the lost language of the mysterious Garamantian kingdom. Other inscriptions found on "Inscription Mountain" had ancient Egyptian influence mixed with what may have been Ammonian, for we saw snakes and other animals similar to those depicted on hieroglyphics.

There was much work to be done here, but summer was now coming on and we had regretfully to bid farewell to the Oasis of Jupiter-Ammon and to its mysterious half-buried ruins in the surrounding oases, its legendary lakes and haunted islands, its vast regions of unknown dawn-men, its temples and mountains of mummies, and other relics of the Ammonian kingdom.

Farewell, also, to a strange and dying Siwan people, primitive children of the desert, who with all your failings and shortcomings are, after all, part of us, linked with human bindings. May your half starved and sickened bodies, like those of your stronger yet disappearing brothers, the Tuareg, be succored by what civilization can bring you. Perhaps some of those in more prosperous lands may hear your dying call and come to help you, to relieve you a little of the sickness and misery that come from such utter poverty and life in such barren lands. I have promised to tell them of your struggles and sufferings, of the premature death of your children from want and sickness. Perchance the words, taken through lands flowing with milk and honey, shall not go unheeded. Perchance the day will yet dawn when the feelings of the great hearted ones will respond to your cry and save the last remnants of a once great people. Perchance.

Our hearts were touched when we left our camp on the sides of the silent Djebel Muta and turned our faces to distant civilization. We had made good friends of our poor Siwan servants, and they made a pathetic little group around the cars as we made ready to go. A few months of kindness and gifts of clothes, a little medicine, and even toys, had endeared them.

I could not find Ali-Ford among them, but going into the fly-filled "kitchen" I found him sobbing his heart out in a dark corner. Amid his wailings we were told that for the first time in his bitter life a few kindnesses had been bestowed on him and that now the hour had struck when he was again to be treated as a dog. Poor Ali! We shall never forget your accent, taught by the British Tommies in the recent desert war around Siwa, and we will long remember your great love for driving a Ford, especially into trees, and your drinking of unlimited *lubki* mixed with gasoline – the Siwan cocktail!

To assuage Ali's grief we gave him the small collapsible Christmas tree with its silver trappings, which friends had sent us. This consoled him a little, and the promise of a phonograph cheered him a little more. Amid sobs he told us that all there was left for him to do was to get married again! He was only nineteen years old and had already been divorced four times. When we asked him if he had anyone in view he said, rather sadly, "Yes, I'll take back my third wife. After all, she was the best of the lot."

A simple desert child, with his love for a spangled Christmas tree and a wife who had been a little better than the others.

As we reached the great precipices that tower above the magic, lovely oases, we gave one last look on what had been our desert home. A Saharan dawn was illuminating the vari-colored, wild mountains; the early sun rays were lighting the fields of palm trees with a golden touch; delicate purple shadows were turning into amber amid the silent canyons and the lakes were beginning to reflect the turquoise depths of the star-dying heavens. Like a mirage the rock of Agourmi was appearing above the lake reflected palms. It was the last vision we had of the hero-haunted land of the Ammonians.

With the memories of the mighty past came the realization that we were going back to the civilized world, with its fevers and smallness, its petty jealousies and the nerve-wracking struggle to keep one's head upstream. Do you wonder that we left the peace and the loveliness of it all with a sigh of regret and a tear? We had come to love those great silences. The stones of the golden temples had spoken to us in a language of their own. The legends and histories had lived within us again. Alexander the Great, the now voiceless Oracles, Herodotus, lovely Fountain of the Sun, the purple and crimson sunsets and even poor insignificant Ali-Ford, were now but memories of a glorious adventure.

Great indeed is the fascination of archaeological exploration, the discovering of lost and forgotten people, the linking up of civilizations thousands of miles apart, and finding of coins, inscriptions, and human artifacts that give us dates and historical information. The prehistoric sites of the Nubian and Libyan Deserts have now been linked with the great similar neolithic chain of remains of prehistoric men from the Nile and Faiyum Oasis to Southern Tunisia, Algeria and Morocco, and our coming expedition will continue the search into the unexplored regions of Rio Del Oro and Mauretania.

Did these "makers of the wonderful flints" reach even further – to the Americas, where the worked flints are identical to those found in the Southern States of America and in Mexico? Perchance the last link in the chain is to be found in the great deserts and mountains of the Rio Del Oro and Mauretania or, perhaps, it lies forever hidden at the bottom of the wide Atlantic. It will be thrilling if we can come upon these links along these desolate, unexplored coasts of Rio Del Oro – links that will bind up three thousand five hundred miles of Saharan exploration.

Now the tale is nearly told. You have followed our expeditions to abandoned cities, and to explore romantic traces of past and forgotten peoples. We have taken you among the living peoples of Africa, whose ancestors built the marvelous palaces and tombs that make a golden trail from the Atlantic to the Nile. The pickax and shovel, the powerful motor car and groups of earnest scholars, have revealed a few of the secrets of the Great Desert.

The history of Egypt has been laid bare, but to the west there are still great realms and problems to be solved by scientific exploration. The surface only has been scratched. Great explorers, such as Barth and Duveyrier, have left splendid accounts of their traversing unknown regions, but in passing through they may have passed a rich tomb or an entire dead city within a few miles of the trail they blazed. A region should be systematically explored if we are able to say "that region is known."

Our preliminary survey of North Africa tells us that, geographically, there are various regions yet to be explored, especially south of Siwa and between the mountains of Tibesti and the Nile. Rohlfs, in 1874, explored between Siwa and west of the Dakhla Oasis; several hundred miles are unknown between his old trail and that of Hassanein Bey in 1923. Prince Kernel-el-Din, in 1925-26, explored the region of Gebel Owenat and Sarra, where Bruneau de Laborie passed in 1923 on his way to Kufara.

The whole northern part of the great Tibesti Mountains shows white on the map, unknown and totally unexplored. The Tilho expedition went south of Tibesti in 1914, but there are several hundred miles between these savage mountains and the great Hoggar range still to be trod by the feet of the explorer.

My life ambition has been to cross the Sahara from the Atlantic to the Red Sea, taking in the last unexplored regions of the world's greatest desert. The trail would take us through the unknown Rio Del Oro (to which we are now on the point of leaving to make a preliminary survey), then through the vast unmapped region called the Djouf – twelve hundred miles of unmapped territory! Thence the way would lead on to Taodeni, and across the desolate Tanezrouft to the Hoggar. In these mountains we shall excavate the large tombs noticed in 1925, and complete the exploration of the other chambers of the sepulchre of Queen Tin Hinan.

South of the Hoggar we shall explore the lost city of Tokalet, said to be on the unmapped river called Oed Tafassasset. The Tuareg are convinced of the existence of this lost oasis and ruined city, which they have heard of from their ancestors. Emeralds and gold dust, they say, came from there. Who knows but that it may be the famed mines of the Garamantians?

Tibesti is still to add many a page to the geographical, ethnographical and archaeological history of the world, and I have already spoken of the new trail that we shall blaze across the blazing waste of the Libyan deserts. From the Nile we shall pass to the Red Sea, across an unknown part of the Libyan Desert, ancient Berenice – a challenging adventure of five thousand miles! King Fuad of Egypt notified us of his interest in the project and has communicated to the Royal Egyptian Geographical Society that the arrival of the Franco-American Trans-Saharan Expedition from the Atlantic to the Red Sea will be the occasion of the opening of the new Institute of the Sahara!

The archaeological researches are just as important as the geographical knowledge yet to be gleaned. The summer palace of Queen Cleopatra at Mersa Matru is still a field for future discoveries. The Temple of Jupiter-Ammon still contains the undiscovered treasure of the priests of old. The Isle of Djerba, once the home of Homer's "Lotus Eaters," bears seven dead cities, whilst the area in the vicinity of where Cato died at Utica, is still virgin soil for the excavator.

The archaeological cities of North Africa are like a vast open-air museum. From Volubilis in Morocco, to golden

Gigthis on the lesser Syrtian Sea, there is one golden chain of silent, magnificent ruins. My own eyes have beheld the remains of three hundred forgotten sites – a rich field for many years of thrilling research.

The vast prehistoric regions of North Africa have been only scratched on the surface. The great desert still holds many historical treasures testifying to the existence of mighty kingdoms. There are still the strange, mysterious tombs at Ghadames, the ancient capital of the Garamantians; there are the tombs and ruins to be explored in the mysterious Hoggar and in unknown Mauretania, and north of the savage Adrar there are the remains of nameless empires.

There is a lure and thrill in the exploration of these desert places. One longs for the moment when all preparations are finished and the trail is open before you – "the out-trail, the long trail, but the trail that is always new."

The spirit of exploration is not new. Hundreds of years before Christ the ancient Carthaginians explored the desolate coasts of Southern Morocco, Rio Del Oro and Mauretania, where we are now wending our steps. Larach (el Araish) the Arabs call it, is identified with the famed gardens of the Hesperides with its golden apples. Several miles south of the Pillars of Hercules (Gibraltar) are the ruins of the Carthaginian colony of Azemour, while in the "Periplus" of Hanno we read of strange adventures and mysterious lands that lured the fearless Phoenicians centuries before Christ. We know that the Nasamones crossed the Sahara from Carthage, that the Roman Balbus penetrated far into the desert, and we know, too, of the magnificent exploit of Septimus Flaccus, who reached Agisymbo Regio, the Air of to-day, 100 B. C.

Ah, the lure of the Sahara is enduring! There is something magnetic in the desire to reach the weird volcanic mountains of the Hoggar and Tibesti. Once you have seen the sunset on the majestic dunes of the Libyan Desert, you will yearn to enjoy that thrill again. The Saharan nights, passed by some lonely Tuareg camp fire, are hours that you would live over many times again. There is an eager haste to go back. Like the glorious desert sunset, the pictures begin to fade. One imagines once more the Great Ones of the Past thundering into the night – Hannibal, Alexander, Scipio Africanus, Kahena, Massinissa, heroes of Old Africa, phantoms of epic tales, who are little more than legends now. . .

As the twilight darkens the flitting pictures pass by, presenting momentary visions of the lands of the Troglodytes, the weird tom-toms beating in Siwa Town; the strange madness of the fanatical Aissaoua and the majesty of the veiled Tuareg, passing across the horizon of their wild lands.

Romance and memory – these are the tinted veils drawn at evening between our vision and the trials, the heat and the hardships; the fevered quest of the glaring day. Well we know that to-morrow the urge to go on will drive us forth again with eyes intent on the tasks at hand, with thoughts trained sharply forward attempting to foresee what dangers lie waiting in the burning sands ahead.

But the Saharan night "drops her curtain down, and pins it with a star." Mountains, sand dunes, golden oases, forgotten ruins and endless trails go trooping through the halls of memory. In the distance one hears the soft notes of a desert flute coming out of the cool, dim recesses of a magical oasis. It speaks of fierce passions, of vague longings and of the lure of the vast desert spaces which man, "in search of a word," has called – Sahara. . .

"'So on, ever on, spreads the path of the Desert,
Wearily, wearily,
Sand, ever sand – not a gleam of the fountain;
Sun, ever sun – not a shade from the mountain;
As a sea on a sea flows the width of the Desert
Drearily, drearily. . .'"

BIBLIOGRAPHY

Augieras, E .... *Le Sahara Occidental, 1919.*

Barth, H .... *Travels and Discoveries in* North and Central Africa, London, 1852-1853.

Ball, J .... *Problems of the Libyan Desert, R. G. J., July, 1927.*

Bazin, R .... *Life of Charles de Foucauld, London, 1923.*

Beadnell .... *The Sand Dunes of the Libyan Desert.*

Beadnell .... *The Libyan Desert Oasis Series.*

Belgrave, D .... *Siwa.*

Bissuel........................... *Les Tuaregs de l'Oest.*

Boissier, G..................... *l'Afrique Romaine, Paris, 1901.*

Browne, W. C................ *Travels in Africa (1792-6).*

Buchanan, A .... *Sahara, 1925.*

Budge............................ *Life of Alexander.*

Cailliaud........................ *Travels in the Oases.*

Chevrillon, A .... *Puritans of the Desert (Mzab), 1927.*

Chudeau, R., and Gautier, E. L *Missions au Sahara et Soudan, Paris, 1908.*

Cortier........................... *D'Une Rive a l'autre du Sahara, Paris, 1908.*

Denham-Clapperton...... *Travels and Discoveries in Central Africa, 1826.*

Dumichen, I .... *Die Oasen der Libische Wuste.*

Duveyrier, H .... *Exploration du Sahara, Two Vol., Paris, 1804.*

Duveyrier, H .... Edmonstone's Journey, 1822.

Falls, E .... *Three Years in the Libyan Desert.*

Flamand .... *Les Pierres Ecrits.*

Forbes, R....................... *The Secret of the Sahara, Kufara.*

Gautier, E. F................. *La Conquete du Sahara, Paris, 1919.*

Gautier, E. F .... *Le Sahara, Paris, 1923.*
Gradis, G .... *A La Recherche du Grand Axe, 1923.*
Gsell, S .... *Histoire Ancienne de L'Afrique du Nord, Vol. 1 to 5, Paris, 1920.*
Hamilton, J .... *Wanderings in North Africa.*
Hornemann, F. C .... *Journal, from Cairo to Mouzouk.*
Hume, W. F .... *Geology of the Eastern Desert, Cairo, 1907, and divers works by this author.*
Kerillis, H. de .... *De l'Algerie au Dahomey, Paris, 1924.*
King, H .... *Mysteries of the Libyan Desert, 1925.*
Largeau, V .... *Le Sahara, Paris, 1877.*
Lenz, O .... *Timbucktu to Morocco, 1884.*
Lyon, G. F .... *Travels in North Africa, 1821.*
Martin, A. G. P .... *Les Oases Sahariennes, 1908.*
Morgan de, Captain .... *Gobert, Flamand, Prorok, and Pallary.*
Nachtigal, G .... *Sahara and Soudan, Berlin, 1881.*
Parhey, C .... *Der Orakel und die Oase des Ammons.*
Pervinquires, L .... *"Gadames," Paris, 1912.*
Prorok, B. de .... *Ancient Trade Routes of the Sahara, A. G. J., 1925.*
Prorok, B. de .... *The Temple of Tanit Carthage, Smith. Inst., 1920.*
Reygasse, M .... *Divers Publications on the Prehistory of North Africa.*
Richardson, J .... *Travels in the Great Desert of Sahara, London, 1847.*
Rohlfs, G .... *Quer durch Africa.*
St. Martin .... *Nord de l'Afrique en Antiquite.*
Schirmer, H .... *Le Sahara, 1892.*
Schweinfurth .... *Aufnahmen in der Ostlichen Wuste, Berlin, 1900.*
Schweinfurth .... *Auf Unbetretenen Wegen, Hamburg, 1922.*
Vischer, H .... *Across the Sahara, 1910.*
Weisgerber, H .... *Les Blancs d'Afrique.*
White, S .... *From Sphinx to Oracle, 1900.*

CLASSICAL AND ARABIAN AUTHORS

Abu el Hassan
Ali Mas'udi .... *Harvard Studies.*
Corippus .... *Works.*

Herodotus...................... *Geography.*
Ibn Khaldun .... *"History of the Berbers, Algiers, 1852.*
Juvenal .... *Satires.*
Leo Africanus .... *Africae Descriptio.*
Pindar........................... *Hymns to Deities.*
Pliny............................. *Natural History.*
Plutarch........................ *Life of Alexander.*
Ptolemy........................ *Geography.*
Sallustius...................... *DeBello Jurgurthino.*
Siculus.......................... *The Works of Diodorus Siculus.*
Silius Italicus .... *Complete Works.*
Strabo........................... *Geography.*
Virgil .... *Aeneid.*

Afterword

THE LIFE AND DEATH OF BYRON KHUN DE PROROK

by Michael Tarabulski

They say all lovers swear more performance than they are able, and yet reserve an ability that they never perform: vowing more than the perfection of ten; and discharging less than the tenth part of one. They that have the voice of lions, and the act of hares: are they not monsters?

Shakespeare,
Troylus and Cressida, III: ii

Dear beloved Byron has gone," said James B. Pond, editor of *Program Magazine*, writing in the November-December issue about the death of Byron Khun de Prorok. "In late November he was found in a dying condition on a railway train in France. He was taken to a hospital in Paris where he passed away on November 21st"

He should have had a State funeral. He was picked up alone, in trouble, almost unknown. Obituaries, funeral orations, are things of little moment. Byron needed them not. Forever in the memories of those who knew him will be something that will endure as long as mortals endure. He was loved. Can one say more?

One can. I have been looking into the facts and the fictions of Byron's life for over two decades and I've learned that for every reaction to him there is an equal but opposite reaction. "Of the dead," goes Roman wisdom, "speak no ill." Were I to do that, I'd only tell you half of this tale. To those whom the whole of it brings pain—and there will be at least two such—I offer my apologies. Those who saw only his public face, as a travel lecturer or the author of books and articles on his adventures, often admired him. Those who knew him only professionally, for his archaeological work, often reviled him. Those who knew him well often shared the sentiments of both camps.

If ever you have loved someone but could not bear to be around that person because his or her irresponsible, unreliable, and undependable behavior threatened your mental health and physical safety, then you can stop reading right now. If you've had that experience, then you have known Byron and reading what follows will be redundant if not painful. On the other hand, if you have not had that experience, or if you have had it and you believe that every unhappy story is unhappy in its own way, read on.

We begin at the end of *this* unhappy story on a train, not under one, with de Prorok dead in Paris in November, 1954, at age 58. The Foreign Service "Report on the Death of an American Citizen" gives the cause of death as "intoxication following absorption of an overdose of Nembutal." He was just concluding a travel lecture tour.

Here's more from his *Program Magazine* obituary:

> One might use the word *flamboyant* in connection with
> him. Byron de Prorok was one of the rare personages of
> our times: handsome, highly intelligent, possessed of
> great platform ability. Everyone who knew him loved
> him. [Original emphasis.]

*On the lecture platform he was a supreme favourite.
Year after year he went back to the same places. Each
year he turned up some new subject. At his beginning,
he lectured with old 35mm black and white movies. At
the end he was using 16mm color movies. Throughout
his career he never learned the slightest thing about
motion pictures. He never knew whether they were good
or bad (they were often atrocious), upside down, or
hind side to. It made no difference. Audiences loved the
man who, regardless of the film, poured out fascinating
information that made other ages come to life, that
instilled vitality into the places and people who passed
on his screen. People forgot the pictures, in the man.
His knowledge of almost everything was near to super-
human.*

Comments from the fictional funeral of another desert
adventurer, also dead through carelessness, come to mind.
"Yes, it was my privilege to know him...and to make him
known to the world," says the Lowell Thomas character,
Jackson Bentley (Arthur Kennedy), in bombastic reply to a
reporter's question at the State funeral of the eponymous
hero of Lawrence of Arabia, "He was a poet, a scholar, and a
mighty warrior." But, when the reporter moves away, Bentley speaks to a companion in cynical sotto voce: "He was
also the most shameless exhibitionist since Barnum and
Bailey."

I first heard about Byron in April of 1982. I was in my
final semester at Beloit College and had traveled to northern
Wisconsin to meet with Alonzo Pond (no relation to James
B.), then 89 years-old. Beloit's Logan Museum of Anthro-
pology had a collection of ethnological materials, and
accompanying documentation in the form of reports, photographs, and film, relating to a 1925 expedition into the
Sahara. Alonzo Pond and another Beloit alumnus, Bradley
Tyrrell, had been on that expedition, in Byron's company,

and had assembled the collection. These materials interested me and I jumped at the chance to meet with Pond.

So it was that I found myself with him, asking about the other members of the expedition. Along with Tyrrell and de Prorok were Maurice Reygasse, an Algerian government functionary and amateur archaeologist; Hal Denny, from the New York Times; Louis Chapuis, a guide; Caid Belaid, an interpreter; Henri Barth, a cameraman; and three drivers. De Prorok had definitely made an impression: "He was the most charming man I ever met," Pond told me, "but I don't think he himself knew what part of what he said was true and what part false."

De Prorok was given to making up answers on the spot, Pond said, in matters simple and complex. Serious omissions in camping supplies had already alerted Pond that de Prorok was weak on details, so before leaving Constantine for Batna, Pond asked him if the three cars had been properly fueled. De Prorok replied that they had been. Late in the day, two cars ran out of gas. During and after the six week trip, when issuing progress reports, Byron greatly exaggerated the hardships endured and the discoveries made by the expedition. Moreover, he left Algeria with archaeological materials he was not supposed to take. When I laughed at Pond's stories, out of sheer astonishment at de Prorok's chutzpah, he upbraided me. "It's not funny," he said, "we could've died! As it was, he got us into a lot of trouble. But he could say *anything* and, if you didn't know better, you'd believe him. Good God, even if you *did* know better you'd half believe him until you thought about it for a while. That was the wonder of the man."L. Sprague de Camp, in *Lost Continents: The Atlantean Theme in History, Science, and Literature* (1954), summarizes Byron's career. "De Prorok started out as a competent archaeologist who did sound work on the site of Carthage. Later he seems to have gone in for a type of exploration that, if it produced less substantial

scientific returns, provided him with adventure and furnished lively copy for his books."

Others characterize him less generously. Anthropologist
L. Cabot Briggs said this of de Prorok in a 1973 letter to
Andrew Whiteford at the Logan Museum:

> *He was a distinctly dubious character, and pulled the
> wool over the eyes of Reygasse very effectively (and of
> quite a lot of other people too....). When I was a boy, I
> was taken to a lecture he gave at the Fogg Art Museum
> at Harvard (on the subject of his excavations at
> Carthage). I remember that he used as a pointer a very
> long ebony cane with an elaborate silver knob, the kind
> the dandies at the court of Louis XIV used to strut
> around with.*
>
> *He was that kind of guy.*

Or take this *Boston Transcript*, January 4, 1936, review
of *In Quest of Lost Worlds*:

> *The author speaks with kindly condescension of the well
> founded camps of the more pedestrian scientists who
> spend years in excavating a single site and in making
> painstaking reports. The reader gets the general
> impression that anybody can do that. This blasé attitude
> is doubly unfortunate because so much of his material,
> especially that dealing with Ethiopia and Central
> America, is of such fascinating interest that the reader
> would be held spellbound if he weren't continually irri-
> tated by Prorok's literary gaucheries.*

But the *New York Times* review of January 19, 1936,
praises the same book:

Vividly told, this record of strange adventure and stranger discoveries is positively breath-taking, and the reader who has followed with tense absorption every word of the extraordinary narrative closes it feeling that the thing more amazing than any other is the fact that the count survived to write of his experiences.

Bradley Tyrrell, fresh from the Sahara expedition, equivocates in a diary entry written in Paris on December 8, 1925:

Prorok is a charming fellow - but flighty - he is an adventurer with a rich smattering of history & language - a title - a love of decorations and I think a sincere desire to add something to science, but without the guts to dig through the details necessary. He has brilliant ideas - enormous conceptions - at times- but is apt to go on to something 'new' before the old is even well started. Science is classified knowledge - but he will always need people willing to do his 'classifying.' He needs a balance wheel - more than that perhaps - a boss - a manager who can keep his feet on the ground. With that there is no end to the delightful dips he may take into the fringes of history and science - and the world will give him a hearing!

Back in Beloit, Logan Museum Director George Collie was less sanguine. De Prorok had been presenting himself as working for the museum. This from a letter of December 10, 1925:

Personally I have no use for de Prorok and I know that a good many of the American archaeologists feel the same way. He is an advertiser and exploits the things he finds and tries to make money off of them apparently. He is in no way connected with the college and must not be so regarded....

The National Geographic Society had the same problem with de Prorok much later, in 1948. He appeared in Morocco and claimed to be making a film for them. L. Cabot Briggs, cited above, reported this news to the NGS and the society notified Moroccan authorities that de Prorok was not in their employ. However, an Internal Memo from Gilbert Grosvenor to J.O.L., dated 14 July 1925, shows that the Society did give him a chance:

Regarding Prorok: I agree with you that he is an unusually clever "personal press agent," social and otherwise, etc. But he is also a good organizer and has stirred up so much interest in Carthage and North African ruins that he has gathered into his project [the] ablest archaeologists of the United States and France.

But Byron would promise more than he could carry out, or go back on his promises. Grosvenor continues:

The last time he came to Washington the date was made six months in advance, with the understanding that it would be his only lecture, but, to my surprise, Mitchell Carroll arranged for Prorok to address the Archaeological Society the day before the National Geographic Society. Prorok should have known better. When I called him to task for doing this, he stated that he did not accept Carroll's invitation until he was assured by Carroll that the National Geographic Society had no objection.

Sorting out the Sahara expedition mess, Sheldon Whitehouse, Chargée d'Affaires at the American Embassy in Paris, in a June 4, 1926, letter back to the Department of State, wrote: "Prorok is a scatter-brained jackass and ought to have a nurse...."

[He] left a trail of unpaid bill behind him in Algeria, but these have now been settled and the Governor General of Algeria has withdrawn any complaint against him. He has, however, tangled matters up frightfully by enlisting the aid of Madame Rouvier, the widow of the former Premier, in obtaining the permit he now desires for the galley at Carthage. Madame Rouvier, who is not in the slightest degree interested in archaeology, naturally wanted a quid pro quo and asked Prorok to sell some antique furniture for her in America, which he said he would do. Madame Rouvier then got very busy, made various trips to the Foreign Office and apparently has got the permit, or the assurance of a permit, in her pocket. As Prorok did nothing about her furniture and apparently considered it a matter of no importance, she is very angry....

Yet, in a page two item of February 17, 1926, the *New York Times* said:

Count Byron Khun de Prorok, explorer of the buried cities of Northern Africa, lectured at Carnegie Hall last night on his recent discoveries on the sites of ancient civilizations. Introduced by George Palmer Putnam as "a man who has taken archaeology out of the hands of the graybeards," the count looked hardly older than a boy as he stood on the Carnegie Hall stage and told the dramatic story of his adventures.

More vivid even than his own descriptions was the showing of six thousand feet of motion picture film, illustrating the progress of the expedition on the plains where Hannibal fought Scipio, over the once flourishing submarine city of Djerba, and then inland to the sand wastes of the Sahara and Atlas Mountains....

> *Count de Prorok complained of a real estate boom which was developing on the site of modern Carthage, and which, he said, was making archaeological research there more and more expensive. Real Estate speculators, he said, were buying land under which priceless treasures lie buried and then extorted high prices when the archaeologists began their excavations....*

That apparent concern for the archaeological enterprise, however, didn't translate abroad. Here's an excerpt from an exchange of U.S. Department of State correspondence dated January 26, 1927. Archaeologist Alfred Kidder, then with the National Research Council, had written to Assistant Secretary of State Robert Olds to ask for help in getting his older brother, Homer, permission to do some archaeological work in Algeria. Olds' office wrote this to a Mr. LeClercq in the Division of Western European Affairs:

> *I have written [Alfred] Kidder that we will notify the French Government that his brother, Homer Kidder, is all right. I think this should be done as a matter of routine through the Embassy. We do not, of course have to ask for any special facilities, but with Prorok, and people of his sort, making trouble in North Africa, I am afraid that without a word from the Embassy the French Government will not be friendly toward anything Homer Kidder may want to do.... [Emphasis added.]*

Scatter-brained jackass" in need of a nurse seems a bit harsh but it is clear enough that Byron, shall we say, "had issues." It is true that in correspondence, official and personal, in newspaper accounts, and in his own writings, one sees that behind many of the negative things said about him there might be a more favorable explanation. His financial problems in Tunisia and Algeria might have been due to corrupt officials asking for bribes. The accusation that he stole things from Algeria might have been groundless. Madame Rouvier might have been exploiting him for her own ends. What some considered his scientific failings might more charitably be seen as a desire to make science appealing to a wide audience. And so on. However, taken all in all, and reflecting as they do a constant theme of deceit, the words of his detractors build a case against him. When we add to those the comments of supporters who praise him with faint damns, we may be comfortable in the assumption that the man was not completely misunderstood.

Complete understanding of him is a different matter. How are we to even partially understand the mind and motives of anyone, much less a man now half a century dead? Some clues are offered in what little autobiography he provides in his four books; but which details, in which of his four books, are true and which are false I cannot say.

Nor can I for certain even if he wrote the books himself or had editorial help that amounted almost to ghostwriting, or at least to clandestine co-authorship as in the more recent case of the late Jerzy Kosinski. (An apt analogy, for Kosinski had many versions of his own life story. So, for that matter, did T.E. Lawrence.) Regarding the 1925 "Tin-Hinan" expedition, for example, the writings of Alonzo Pond and Bradley Tyrrell tell a tale different from Byron's, and his own accounts differ from his first rendition of it in *Digging for Lost African Gods* (1926), through *Mysterious Sahara* (1929), to *In Quest of Lost Worlds* (1935). Readers should be on guard: Byron is a delightful but overly-imaginative guide.

Other clues to Byron's life are in the biographical details given in newspapers. Still others exist only as oral testimony (in this case family history) passed along from those who knew him to those who didn't. These varied clues are all we have to work with. Upon them I build the following biography. The conclusion I leap to is my own.

According to a statement in the New York Times of December 28, 1925, Byron was born in Mexico City on 6 October 1896. At birth he was named Francis Byron Khun (or Kuhn). His father was Leonard Khun (or Kuhn), a naturalized American citizen and owner of a large vinegar distillery. His mother was Therese de Prorok. Both were from well-to-do Austro-Hungarian families.

From his daughters I learned that Byron was the oldest of five children, with three brothers and a sister. When he was a boy, Byron's parent separated or divorced. His siblings stayed with their father. Byron lived with his mother and her brother and their mother, an Englishwoman. They lived in France, with one home near Paris and another at the Château de Tancarville, in Normandy, near Le Havre. His uncle, Theophile Konerski de Prorok, adopted him.

At about the age of ten, Byron was packed off to boarding school in England. He attended several schools. His most revealing autobiographical sketch, in *Dead Men Do Tell Tales* (1942), deals with this period of his life. The archaeology and exploration bugs bit him early, and one bright spot in these otherwise miserable years, was a meeting with Ernest Shackleton who came to his school to lecture. Because Byron had done some digging at Roman ruins near the school, he says in all of his four books, he got to meet with Shackleton. He boldly promised money enough for a sled for Shackleton's next attempt to reach the South Pole, and managed to raise it.

In secondary school Byron moved from England to Switzerland, attending first a preparatory school and then the University of Geneva, where he studied archaeology[1]. This led to work in Italy and then in Tunisia. He admits to having little interest in his education until prep school and college but he was an able polyglot. At least bilingual, in French and English, he had some German, Italian, and Spanish in addition to his boarding school Latin and Greek. (His ability to tell the truth in any of these languages is another matter.) Among his hobbies and talents was watercoloring. He illustrated the jacket covers of his first two books and the title cards for his travel lecture films. Around 1908, his painting hobby, and his family wealth, brought him into contact with Robert Lansing, Woodrow Wilson's Secretary of State (1915-1920), on the French Riviera.

Although a U.S. Citizen from birth, Byron may only have visited the U.S. briefly, if at all, before arriving in New York in 1919. In April of 1920, a small display of his watercolors was mounted in the foyer of Washington's Corcoran Gallery under the name F. Byron-Khun. He soon dropped the "Francis" and added "de Prorok." (Late in life he dropped the Khun altogether.) He prefixed the whole with "Count," a title—also dropped later—from Polish nobility, he said, inherited from his adoptive father.

Now began a yearly cycle of excavation in Carthage through the summer and lectures in Europe and North America through the winter. Returning to America for the 1922-23 season, Byron met Alice Kenny, eldest daughter of William F. Kenny, a wealthy New York City contractor. They married in February of 1923, in St. Patrick's Cathedral, with Governors Al Smith, of New York, and Channing Cox, of Massachusetts (friends of the bride's father) in attendance. New York's Archbishop Hayes conducted the ceremony. The Pope sent blessings. Byron had a rich, well-educated, and musically-talented wife. Alice had a titled husband. They made their home in Paris. In short order, they had two daughters, Marie-Thérèse, born in 1924, and Aliska, born in 1925.

---

1. This, as I said, is his own account A biographical sketch of Byron, among the Campbell Bonner papers at the Kelsey Museum in an Arbor, Michigan, written by his friend Fred Singer, states the Byron did not attend the University of Geneva. Instead,"because of ill health," says Singer, Byron went to the Monastery of St. Honorat, near Cannes,in the south of France, where he continued his studies of history and archaeology.

Byron continued his archaeological excavations in Carthage, mostly in connection with Francis Kelsey of the University of Michigan. W.F. Kenny provided some of the funding for this work through 1923 and 1924. By the spring of 1925, though, de Prorok and Kelsey had run afoul of the Tunisian Ministry of Antiquities and further work at Carthage was curtailed. In the disagreement with the Tunisian government, Kenny defended the integrity of his new son-in-law, calling on political contacts in Washington in an effort to secure permission to get Byron back to Carthage later in 1925.

These efforts came to naught and Byron decided to try some exploration in Algeria. This brought him into contact with Alonzo Pond and the Logan Museum and led to troubles already cited. Kenny defended his son-in-law again, in the debacle that arose from the Saharan trip. His letters to Washington, still in Department of State records at the National Archives, show wholehearted support of Byron. Nonetheless, W.F. Kenny was an intelligent man and apparently saw a disturbing pattern in Byron's behavior.

As Kenny family lore has it, W.F. hired a detective agency to check into Byron's background. The agency, so goes the story, found something unpleasant. Perhaps it was infidelity. Perhaps Byron was not the rightful heir to the Polish title and had just made that up. Perhaps it was that Byron's father, Leonard Khun/Kuhn, was "Jewish" (though just as secular as Byron's "Christian" mother). Or perhaps it was that Khun was not his father at all. Again according to family lore, Byron's biological father was not Khun but a man named Oscar Straus.

And who was this Oscar Straus? There were two men of note with that name around 1895, and surviving Kenny family members thought it was the diplomat who was later Theodore Roosevelt's second term Secretary of Commerce. That Oscar Straus lived from 1854 to 1926. Looking into his life I found him an unlikely paternal candidate. Most importantly, I could find no way to connect his social crowd with that of Therese de Prorok. Less meaningful, given the way these things work, he was much older than she and, by the evidence, happily married.

The second Oscar Straus, the Viennese composer who lived from 1870 to 1954, and was just on the cusp of fame in 1895, is a good bet. First, Oscar and Therese moved in the same social circle. And a famously promiscuous circle it was: Think Arthur Schnitzler's bed hopping play, *Riegen* (1896), made into the film *La Ronde* (1950), with music by...Oscar Straus. Second, the Kenny family story has it that Therese left Europe, for Mexico, already pregnant, and married there. Third, Oscar Straus had just married, in 1895, to his first wife, Helene Neumann, also already pregnant. Finally, photographs of Straus and de Prorok show a startling resemblance: Both have the same tall, lanky build, high forehead, dark, curly hair, and prominent nose.

This is far from conclusive proof, I realize, and there are no rumors of Straus having fathered an illegitimate child. But it is unclear whether or not Therese ever made any claim on Straus. All we do know is that Leonard Khun, for some reason, separated from his wife and that she took this one child, of four, back to Europe. There, her brother adopted him. Among the Tuareg of the Sahara it is the rule that the mother's brother play social father to his sister's children. In our culture it is exceptional.

Returning to the realm of fact, we find that, in the fall of 1926, Alice de Prorok took the two little girls and returned to her parents' home in New York. She never went back to Byron. They were divorced the following July. Byron wrote her during the separation period. These letters make it clear that Byron's heavy drinking contributed to the break-up but also hint at something deeper. Writing on December 5, 1926, he says:

*Am leaving this evening , & am thinking of last year
when I left with Brad [Tyrrell] full of hope & and ambition, and the joy of adventure—and this year, alone,
broken, ill & feeling like an old man. Mother last night
said that she would swear or sign a document to the
effect that I never knew those certain things that it was
said this summer I did know. But what is past is past & I
hope that those that would not believe me are content.
They would be if they saw me now. [Original empha-
sis.]*

Taking this to mean that the detectives uncovered the
secret of Byron's birth and made it known to Kenny, and that
word of it then came to Byron, one can imagine the shock.
He might have suspected something because of his separation from his father and siblings and his adoption by his
maternal uncle, but by evidence of this letter—if we are to
believe it—he did not know he was illegitimate until he was
29 years-old.

After their daughter's divorce, William Kenny and his
wife, Mary, adopted her two daughters and changed their
surnames to Kenny and their given names to Maureen and
Denise. Later, when Alice remarried, her new husband
adopted the girls. Though Byron and Alice met at least once,
years later, he and his two daughters never had direct contact
again. He dedicated his *In Quest of Lost Worlds* to them—as
Maureen and Denise de Prorok. Alice always spoke well of
Byron, and of her time with him. The girls, growing up, had
some limited contact with Byron's brothers and sister and
others who knew him.

Byron remarried shortly after the divorce. The "companion on my recent expedition," of the introduction to *Mysterious Sahara*, is this second wife. They had a son together. He
died at about age ten. This marriage broke up and Byron
married again, around 1940, to a woman named Muriel Ivy.

She survived him and died in Lausanne, Switzerland, in 1990, a fact I only learned of in 2002.

The question of Byron's parentage is important here, even as it was important for his close contemporary in so many things, T. E. Lawrence. In response to his troubles and his critics, he might have turned totally legitimate—such was within his grasp—but the revelation of "those certain things" and the loss of his wife and children in 1926 may have destroyed any pretensions he had of being "legitimate" in any sense. Or maybe he was just a big jerk. I don't know. What is clear is that after 1926 his work never had even the marginal credibility of the Tunisian and Algerian projects. (Some sources, none official, say he was a Colonel in a special desert unit of the U.S. Army in World War II.) By his post-1926 work he lost what respect he'd had in the archaeological community, but his wild stories sold in bookstores and on the lecture circuit. What happened to Byron Khun de Prorok? I think it was a mixture of personal loss and popular approval.

The issue of living within the stereotype of the archaeologist, and attracting fame and (relative) fortune, or taking arms against it and being considered irrelevant, is not so very different in our day than it was in Byron's. Modern archaeological museums and magazines rely upon ancient glitz and glamour to attract funding and subscribers. To paraphrase what has been said of university presidents: Many a museum director has entered that post a scholar and left it a showman; some do not suffer the original burden. The romance of archaeology catches the student's eye and mind and is mother to the amateur and the professional alike; only the wisest know who their father is. Perhaps, feeling no real identity of his own, Byron became what the public saw him as: a drawing room explorer and matinee idol archaeologist. Society made him, as much as it makes any of us. If not really a count, he was surely an heir of Baron Munchausen and, as Irving Howe said of T.E.

Lawrence, a prince of our disorder. He was loved. He still is. Can one say more?

Acknowledgements and Sources

Contemplating the life of Byron makes a person appreciate family. I thank my wife, Sheila O'Brien, and our daughter, Lillian, for their patience when I was lost in the lives of another man and wife and their girls.

I would not have written this brief summary of de Prorok's life if it had not been for William Urschel and The Narrative Press so thoughtfully resurrecting Byron's books. I could not have written it without the help of the following people and institutions:

First and foremost, his daughters, Maureen and Denise, shared with me the information, and documents, that their mother, Alice, had passed along to them. Their cousin, Peter, supplied his memories, admittedly hazy, of old family stories. I hope I have done justice to all and betrayed no trusts.

John Tyrrell helped me to transcribe his father's 1925 trip diary. Thanks, John.

Thanks to Jane Ketcham and Nicolette Meister, former and current Collections Managers of the Logan Museum, and to Fred Burwell, Beloit College Archivist. Renee Braden, National Geographic Society; Sarah Demb, formerly of Harvard's Peabody Museum; Milt Gustafson, NARA-Archives II; Kathryn Hodson, University of Iowa; Don Lennon, East Carolina University; Robin Meador-Woodruff, Kelsey Museum of Archaeology; and Irena Murray, McGill University, each sent me a piece of this Osiris. Ann Owen Wearmouth and Jeanine Miedzwiecki, nature goddesses, gave me the suture to sew him back together. As always, parts are still missing.

The New York Times covered de Prorok's activities throughout the 1920s. The Times sent reporter Harold "Hal" Denny with de Prorok to cover the 1925 expedition. There are many articles about that trip and the subsequent scandal. A reference librarian at any major library can help you find these articles on microfilm or in electronic form. That same librarian can help you find his numerous magazine articles from his North African years, 1920-1930. Most of these are in Art and Archaeology Magazine. The fine librarians at the University of Idaho Library helped me find these and more occult Byronia. Standout help came from Jennifer O'Laughlin, Interlibrary Loan; and Donna Hansen (Ret.), Maria Jankowska, and Diane Prorak, Reference. Diane's family surname used to be Prorok; we could prove no family tie. Incidentally, Prorok, in Polish, means "prophet," as in "A prophet without honor."

Byron's own papers, films, and artifacts from his pre-World War II career were lost in France during that war. The loss of these materials compounds the tragedy of his life. If extant, they would show places and peoples that few but Byron saw fit to record.

Alonzo Pond's personal papers are in the State Historical Society of Wisconsin, in Madison. Records relating to his work for the Logan Museum are in the archives of the Logan Museum and the College Archives at Beloit College, as are Bradley Tyrrell's diary, scrap book, and "home movie" of the 1925 expedition. Additional materials, and copies of some of the materials mentioned above, are at the Human Studies Film Archives of the Smithsonian Institution, Suitland, Maryland, and in the Archives of the American Museum of Natural History in New York City.

THE NARRATIVE PRESS
TRUE FIRST-PERSON HISTORICAL ACCOUNTS

THE HISTORICAL ADVENTURE AND EXPLORATION SERIES

The *Historical Adventure and Exploration Series* from The Narrative Press are all first-hand reports written by the explorers, pioneers, scientists, mountain men, prospectors, spies, lawmen, and fortune hunters themselves.

Most of these adventures are classics, about people and places now long gone. They take place all over the world – in Africa, South America, the Arctic and Antarctic, in America (in the Old West and before), on islands, and on the open seas.

Some of our authors are famous – Ernest Shackleton, Kit Carson, Henry Stanley, David Livingston, William Bligh, John Muir, Richard Burton, Elizabeth Custer, Teddy Roosevelt, Charles Darwin, Osborne Russell, John Fremont, Joshua Slocum, William Manley, Tom Horn, Philip St. George Cooke, Apsley Cherry-Garrard, Richard Henry Dana, Jack London, and Buffalo Bill, to name a few.

One thread binds all of our books: every one is historically important, and every one of them is fascinating.

Visit our website today. You can also call or write to us for a free copy of our printed catalogue.

THE NARRATIVE PRESS
P.O.BOX 2487
SANTA BARBARA, CALIFORNIA 93120 U.S.A.
(800) 315-9005
www.narrativepress.com